Body Image in the Primary School

- The average child watches between 20,000 and 40,000 adverts a year.
- Girls as young as 6 are cutting down on what they eat in order to stay thin.
- Three quarters of 10 to 11-year-olds would like to change their appearance.

The impact of body image on self-esteem has been recognised as an issue which affects increasingly younger children. Research in this area has traditionally focused on adolescents, yet anxieties about appearance often develop at a much earlier age than this. Primary schools have a critical role in helping children to develop a healthy body image through positive intervention.

Body Image in the Primary School offers step-by-step lessons for teachers to address this issue. It examines the continuous media and peer pressures that young children are exposed to and encourages children to recognise their own strengths and qualities and to become resilient members of society. The authors demonstrate a practical range of activities and projects for teachers to work with, designed to make them confident in discussing body image in the classroom.

This book offers:

- lesson plans for Key Stage 1, Key Stage 2 and the transition to Key Stage 3
- practical guidance on how to support and involve parents and carers
- analysis on the changing social influences of home life, peer pressure and the media
- overviews of research on the links between body image, academic achievement and emotional well-being.

This book contains explicit links to SEAL and the ECM outcomes and will be of significant interest to all teachers, teaching assistants and practitioners working with primary children.

Nicky Hutchinson and **Chris Calland** work as behaviour specialists and education consultants in and around Bristol. They are both teachers who have many years experience at both primary and secondary level.

D1227636

Body Image in the Primary School

Nicky Hutchinson and Chris Calland

Routledge
Taylor & Francis Group

LONDON AND NEW YORK

This first edition published 2011
by Routledge
2 Park Square, Milton Park, Abingdon, Oxon, OX14 4RN

Simultaneously published in the USA and Canada
by Routledge
270 Madison Avenue, New York, NY 10016

Routledge is an imprint of the Taylor & Francis Group, an informa business

British Library Cataloguing in Publication Data
A catalogue record for this book is available from the British Library

Library of Congress Cataloging-in-Publication Data
Hutchinson, Nicky.
  Body image in the primary school / by Nicky Hutchinson and Chris Calland. — 1st ed.
    p. cm.
  Includes bibliographical references and index.
  1. School children—Great Britain—Psychology. 2. Body image—Study and teaching (Elementary)—Great Britain. 3. Body image in children—Great Britain. 4. Self esteem—Study and teaching (Elementary)—Great Britain. 5. Self-esteem in children—Great Britain. I. Calland, Chris. II. Title.
  LB1117.H97 2011
  372.83—dc22

                                                                2010035616

ISBN13: 978-0-415-56190-7 (hbk)
ISBN13: 978-0-415-56191-4 (pbk)
ISBN13: 978-0-203-83081-9 (ebk)

Typeset in Bembo
by FiSH Book, Enfield

Printed and bound in Great Britain by
CPI Antony Rowe, Chippenham, Wiltshire

Contents

Acknowledgements

We would like to thank the children of St Bernard's Primary School in Bristol for providing the illustrations for this book.

Thanks also to family and friends for all their support and encouragement.

The authors offer training on body image in the primary school: www.notjustbehaviour.co.uk

CHAPTER

Body image

By the time they reach adulthood, ninety-five per cent of women are dissatisfied with their bodies and seven out of ten girls have been on a diet.

Deanne Jade, National Centre for Eating Disorders

The term 'body image' refers to our idea of how our body looks and how it is perceived by others. It is the mental picture that we hold about our physical appearance, and encompasses how we feel about the size, shape, weight and look of our bodies. Our body image is quite independent of our actual size, shape or appearance. Anyone, of any physical description, can have a positive or negative body image. Because our feelings about our bodies are so deeply connected to our overall view of ourselves, having a poor body image is strongly associated with low self-esteem. A negative body image can be linked to mental illnesses such as anxiety and depression, and to the eating disorders anorexia and bulimia nervosa. Obsessive and exhausting over-exercising behaviour, yo-yo dieting, reluctance to socialise, difficulties with relationships and financial problems have all been associated with poor body image.

The ability of a person to enjoy life, form good relationships and make the most of opportunities can be directly affected by their body image. Feeling positive about your body improves your outlook and how you interact with others, and gives you the freedom and confidence to approach new challenges and experiences. Our feelings and attitudes about our bodies and our physical appearance are closely connected to our self-esteem, or how we feel about our whole selves. Self-esteem can be defined as the beliefs and opinions you have of yourself and how you value and respect yourself as a person. Having a positive body image and feeling content about the way we look is a vital part of our overall emotional health and wellbeing.

The leading UK charity for people with eating disorders, Beat, estimates that 1.6 million people in the UK have an eating disorder, of whom 1.4 million are female. The people most at risk of suffering from an eating disorder are young women between the ages of 14 and 25. As many as one in ten secondary school students are likely to be affected. Eating disorders have the highest mortality rate of any mental illness and many young people who develop anorexia or bulimia will suffer serious long-term health consequences. These include bone and joint disorders, growth retardation and fertility problems.

An extreme disorder of body image is known as body dysmorphic disorder. Sufferers worry excessively that some aspect of their appearance is unattractive, although in reality the perceived flaw is non-existent or minimal. They become preoccupied with the imagined defect and this can have a devastating impact on their daily life. In some cases they avoid all social contact and will not leave the house. The condition is thought to affect as many as one in 200 people and often develops in the teenage years.

The standards of beauty portrayed by the media in our western society are narrow and inflexible. Television, mobile phones, magazines, computers and advertising billboards bombard us constantly with images of slim, beautiful people. Because of the media's powerful presence in our lives we see more images of people every day than we do real faces of family and friends. A young person today is thought to be exposed to more images of physical perfection in one day than a young woman one or two generations ago would have seen throughout her entire adolescence. This has the effect of making exceptional good looks seem normal, real and achievable. Many studies show that looking at pictures of slim, beautiful models has a negative impact on body image (Treasure *et al.*, 2008; Groesz *et al.*, 2002). People are adversely affected by the rigid images of beauty that surround them in the media. They measure their own appearance against these high standards of physical perfection. They begin to view their own body negatively and engage in destructive behaviours to try to reach this unrealistic ideal. Females under the age of 19 and those who are already feeling insecure about their bodies are especially vulnerable.

Many research studies point to a direct link between the media's use of thin models and the rise of eating disorders (Lister, 2010). There has been a steady rise in the incidence of anorexia with each decade. Fashionable standards of female beauty became progressively more unrealistic throughout our society during the previous century. In 1917 the 'perfect' woman was 5 feet 4 inches tall and weighed 10 stone. As the twentieth century progressed, the female beauty ideal became thinner and less representative of an average woman. In the 1970s, top models weighed, on average, 8 per cent less than the average woman, whereas in the twenty-first century they weigh 23 per cent less (Derenne and Beresin, 2006). The current fashionable feminine ideal that is peddled by the media is a toned, thin, large-breasted look. This would be a physical impossibility for most women unless they resorted

to plastic surgery. We often hear about celebrities who have 'achieved' a size zero (an English size four). This gives a woman the waist measurement of an average eight-year-old.

The current media ideal is achievable by less than 5 per cent of the population; that is just in terms of size and weight. If you were to add the perfect facial features too, it would be attainable by hardly anyone at all. Anita Roddick, founder of The Body Shop, reminded us that 'there are over three billion women who don't look like supermodels and only eight who do' (Haywood, 2009).

There is growing evidence that larger numbers of males are also suffering from negative body image. This coincides with an increase in the number of adverts and images we see nowadays that focus on the appearance of the male body (Papadopoulos, 2010). Men with a negative body image worry about their weight, body shape and muscle definition. This can lead to eating disorders, social problems, depression, anxiety, withdrawal and obsessive exercising in the gym. Increasing numbers of body-conscious young males are using anabolic steroids to bulk up their physique, which can lead to serious health consequences. Magazines for men on improving their appearance have grown in popularity. Statistics from the British Association of Aesthetic Plastic Surgeons show that there was a marked increase in the numbers of men opting for cosmetic surgery in 2009.

There are unclear statistics on body image amongst ethnic groups in Britain. There is some evidence to suggest that black and Asian women feel happier with their bodies and less pressure to be slim than white women. In general, it seems that there is a more flexible standard of attractiveness and a greater acceptance of different body shapes amongst black people (Altabe, 1996).

It is clear that our media-driven society is causing widespread pressure to conform to a certain image or look. Beautiful bodies sell products and the diet and advertising industries are multi-million-pound concerns. A recent survey by *Grazia* magazine found that 98 per cent of British women dislike their bodies and the average woman worries about her body every 15 minutes. *Psychology Today* magazine reported that of nearly 3,500 women, 24 per cent said they would sacrifice more than three years of their lives to be the weight they wanted (Godson, 2010). In one recent survey, 95 per cent of 16- to 21-year-olds said they would like to change their bodies and two thirds of teenage girls said they would consider plastic surgery (Hopkirk, 2010). Another study of 2,000 people reported that one in ten women say they feel sick when they see a photo of themselves on the social networking site Facebook, and 13 per cent dislike their appearance so much that they avoid being photographed at all (*Daily Telegraph*, 2010).

Relying too much on appearance to define ourselves is likely to result in poor emotional health. Of course, everyone worries about their looks at times, but when it becomes an obsession and begins to damage a person's whole self-perception, it starts to be a problem. Many people now feel that their physical appearance is more impor- tant than their health or any other personal goals or ambitions. The statistics for plastic surgery in Britain continue to rise dramatically with breast augmentation being the most popular procedure. People are increasingly trying to model themselves on a narrow and unrealistic beauty ideal. There is often a feeling, promoted by the media, that this ideal can be achieved by anyone willing to work hard enough for it. When people fail to achieve this look they can feel frustrated and guilty. They connect their inability to match up to these images with failure and poor self-worth. Even celebrities and supermodels often do not look exactly like their printed images, which may have been airbrushed or digitally enhanced. If we attempt to measure up to an impossible image of physical attractiveness we are setting ourselves up to feel dissatisfied and critical of our bodies.

In our image-obsessed culture, with its emphasis on celebrity and fashion, worries about looks, eating problems and weight concerns have become the norm. Body image dissatisfaction is widespread as increasing numbers of both men and women report feeling anxious and unhappy about their physical appearance. It seems that body worries are everyday concerns for many people in Britain, with high numbers of both women and men feeling dissatisfied with their looks.

Children face exposure to the media on a far greater scale than ever before. Their ideas about themselves, their bodies and their place in society are forming and devel- oping. We must ensure that their development is not limited in any way by the restrictive and unrealistic messages about beauty and the ideal body that they encounter daily in the media. This curriculum project is designed to help children form a healthy body image that is a prerequisite for their emotional health and abil- ity to fulfil their potential.

2

Body image in children

It's good to be skinny.

Ruby, aged 6

Most of the research and literature on young people and body image has focused on adolescents. We now know that a negative body image frequently develops at a younger age than this. We often associate body dissatisfaction and eating problems with teenagers, but the roots of these difficulties can be traced back to an earlier time in childhood. Recent studies show that a negative body image often develops during the pre-teen years while children are still at primary school. Children are showing concerns over their physical appearance and body image at an increasingly young age. Education to tackle this problem has to begin in the primary school. Intervention programmes aimed at adolescents may be too late to prevent many young people from developing a negative body image with its associated eating problems, depression, low self-esteem and anxiety.

Research studies

Evidence indicates that children as young as nine and ten years old, and sometimes even younger, are showing a disturbing level of anxiety about their weight and their physical appearance (Papadopoulos, 2010; Schur *et al.*, 2000; Stice *et al.*, 1999; Maloney *et al.*, 1993). One study reported that slightly more than half of all nine-year-olds were not satisfied with their body image (Hill *et al.*, 1992). A wide-ranging survey of 150,000 children in 2008 by Ofsted found that by the age of 10, a third of girls and 22 per cent of boys cited their bodies as their main source of worry. In a study of over 1,000 girls carried out by Girlguiding UK nearly three-quarters of seven- to eleven-year-olds said they would change something about their appearance, and by the ages of 10 and 11, one in eight girls wanted to be thinner. Other studies show that girls as young as six have distorted body images and worry about their weight (Birbeck and Drummond, 2006; BBC, 2007). Research findings report that between 40 and 50 per cent of children under 13 years of age have high rates of body dissatisfaction (Girlguiding UK, 2010; Papadopoulos, 2010). These findings mean that by mid-childhood, concerns about appearance, weight and dieting are the norm, particularly for girls.

The media

Our children's world is saturated with media images. Within each of these images there is an implicit message about ideals, values and expectations. From social networking sites to mobile phones, i-players and computer games, young people are bombarded constantly with images of flawless, beautiful women who are slim yet curvy, and of muscular, toned men. Many young children now have their own televisions and mobile phones. One large study of five- to sixteen-year-olds found that British children are now spending an average of six hours a day looking at screens (BBC, 2009). Footballers' wives, talent show stars and girl pop-band singers, who feature so extensively on television, and in pop videos and celebrity magazines, often possess surgically enhanced breasts and thin bodies. Frequent exposure to films, television and videos featuring idealised images is linked to lower self-esteem, stress, insecurity and negative moods in girls and young women (Field *et al.*, 2005; Papadopoulos, 2010). Girls see these images and compare themselves unfavourably, feeling that they are failing to match up to an ideal. Advertisers take advantage of this insecurity by suggesting that if you buy their product you will be on your way to achieving the desired look. Children face constant exposure to this message because, on average, a child in the UK watches between 20,000 and 40,000 advertisements a year (Compass, 2006).

Children are vulnerable to the messages of advertising not only because of the sheer volume of adverts that they see but also because their level of intellectual development and lack of experience makes them particularly susceptible to commercial persuasion.

Makeover programmes have been popular on television recently. They are usually scheduled at peak viewing times when children are watching and emphasise the importance of looking good. They can sometimes give the misleading impression that cosmetic surgery offers a quick fix for any part of your physical appearance you dislike. Not only that, but the message often seems to be that fixing your appearance will fix everything else too, giving you a happier life. Cosmetic surgery procedures are becoming more common every year. The UK has the highest rate of cosmetic surgery operations in Europe, with increasing numbers of young people opting for surgery. The number of British teenagers undergoing breast augmentation surgery has increased significantly in recent years.

Modern western society

In the past, and in less industrialised societies, a growing child would not be presented with constant visual reminders of their culture's beauty ideal. The people they would see daily would be their family, friends and close community. This would have enabled them to form a more realistic view of people's physical similarities and differences and, because of this, an easier acceptance of their own body. In addition, a person's image or appearance would not have been as important. In our society, girls and, to a lesser extent, boys are under constant media pressure to look perfect. Young people are susceptible to this pressure and begin to judge their growing body and features against those they see constantly in the media. Many people nowadays idolise celebrities. These celebrities, many of whom have had cosmetic surgery, will invariably have spent some time being groomed and prepared for a photoshoot. The resultant image is often digitally altered and airbrushed to create the illusion of perfection. The image we are admiring is not one of reality. There is often an impression that if we try hard enough and buy the right products this look is attainable. When young people feel that they are not matching up to this image they can judge themselves harshly. If they see their appearance as a measure of their value or self-worth, they feel that they are failures or inadequate in some way. Their perceived physical shortcomings can cause great unhappiness and, ultimately, stops them from accepting themselves fully and fulfilling their potential.

Sexualisation

Children are more susceptible to media pressures because they lack the experience and emotional maturity to understand, filter or moderate the messages. Sexualisation has been defined as the 'imposition of adult sexuality onto children and young people before they are capable of dealing with it, mentally, emotionally or physically' (Papadopoulos, 2010). A government report expressed concern that in our highly sexualised society, where provocative images are used to sell everything, girls are picking up the message that not only should they be slim and pretty, but they should also be looking 'hot' or sexy.

More than one in three children name the computer as the possession they could least live without. Use of the internet and computer games now takes up more of children's viewing time than television (BBC, 2009). Around a third of 8- to 11-year-olds have a social networking site and most use the internet for playing games (Papadopoulos, 2010). Many children say that their use of the internet is unsupervised and this puts them at high risk of exposure to sexually inappropriate images and messages. It is not just the internet that puts them at risk; a significant number of computer games also contain highly sexualised material. A recent survey noted that most female characters were portrayed in a sexualised way, with many being scantily dressed, whilst most male characters were portrayed as aggressive. There has been a significant increase in games depicting various forms of sexual abuse or acts of violence (Papadopoulos, 2010).

Weight and eating

There has been much concern about the increasing number of overweight children in Britain and the rise in childhood obesity has attracted much media attention. Unfortunately, this has sometimes resulted in children internalising the thin ideal, and mistakenly believing that they are overweight. Negative attitudes towards overweight people are formed at a young age. Many children have absorbed the anti-obesity message loud and clear and dread gaining weight, seeing it as something to be avoided at all costs. Research shows that young children are already linking being fat with being unintelligent, doing less well at school, being lazy and smelly and less liked by peers (Bryan, 2003). In contrast, they associate skinny pretty girls with being successful, attractive and having lots of friends. Girls are making a strong connection between happiness and being slim and physically attractive. There is also an assumption that those who are slim and pretty will also be good at other skills like reading, writing and sport (Girlguiding UK, 2009). Some young children who want to be 'skinny' are, by the age of 6, already believing themselves to be too fat and are seeing their bodies as larger than they really are (Schur et al., 2000).

Many more children under the age of 12 are being treated for eating disorders in the UK. The largest eating disorders charity in Britain, Beat, says that professionals are noticing that children are presenting with eating disorders at an ever younger age and they are seeing more cases of anorexia in 8- to 11-year-olds. A comprehensive survey by Girlguiding UK in 2009 found that girls as young as 11 were saying they had to cut down on what they eat to stay thin. Children have reported skipping meals, over-exercising, smoking or using appetite suppressants to lose weight. Unhealthy dieting practices can have serious consequences, not just on children's emotional wellbeing but also on the physical health of growing children. It can put them at risk of restricted growth, delayed puberty, nutrient deficiency and future eating disorders.

Pre-teens

Both boys and girls become more dissatisfied with their appearance between the ages of 10 and 14. Research highlights this age bracket as a high risk period for acquiring a negative body image (Tremblay and Lariviere, 2009). Ofsted (2008) found that whilst a third of girls were worried about their bodies at 10, by the age of 14, half of them cite their figures as their number one worry.

It is at this time, as they approach adolescence, that girls become especially vulnerable to dieting practices. Puberty begins with a growth spurt, and during this stage, for girls, there is also an important increase in body fat tissues. It is during this period of normal weight gain that a negative body image and body dissatisfaction can often begin to develop. At about the age of 10, as children approach the upper end of the primary school, they become more aware of the media and society's values. They often look ahead and take more interest in teenage popular culture. They become more sensitive to media and peer pressures and show a greater desire to 'fit in'. These cultural influences, added to uncertainty about their changing bodies, could be the reason why children in this age range are at such high risk of developing a poor body image.

Girls and boys

In studies of adolescents and younger children, girls consistently show greater concern than boys about their weight and appearance. There is a tendency in our culture for women to be judged and rewarded for their physical attributes, on how pleasing they look to others. Girls receive more messages from their families regarding their weight and looks than do boys, and they are also targeted more by the media.

However, there has been a significant increase recently in the number of males with body image dissatisfaction. Boys worry too about how they look. Whilst girls often want to be thinner, boys are often unhappy with their height and want to be taller. As they get older, boys want to be more muscular. One study demonstrated that both boys and girls wanted to have a body size that was thinner than their own (Skemp et al., 2006). Within the idealised media images of men and women there are strong messages about gender. Females are encouraged to look submissive, young and sexy, whereas men look strong, masculine and powerful. Gender stereotyping can be just as limiting to boys as to girls and can be damaging to healthy, respectful relationships between the sexes.

Although there are differences in the levels of body image concerns between the sexes, research suggests that, to be most effective, curriculum preventative work should be targeted at girls and boys together (Papadopoulos, 2010).

Toys

Children's toys reflect the social values of the culture that they live in. Trends in toys can be seen as markers of underlying social pressures. Barbie's unrealistic body shape, with a large bust, long slim legs and a thin waist and thighs, is reflective of our culture's feminine ideal. If she were a real person it is estimated that she would be over 7 feet tall and measure 36-18-38. These measurements mean that she would lack enough body fat to be fertile. Barbie's body shape creates an unrealistic picture of womanhood for young girls.

The body of Barbie's boyfriend, Ken, has been changed over the last 30 years to become more muscular and well-defined. Other boy dolls, such as Batman, Power Rangers and G.I. Joe, have bulging biceps and measurements that are equally unrepresentative of reality and conform to society's male ideal of a hyper-masculine, honed physique. Toys for personal grooming, such as hair and nail accessories, make-up kits and girly Disney Princess dolls, represent very conventional ideas about femininity. They all emphasise the importance of physical appearance and making efforts to look good.

Other toys have had an inappropriately sexual theme. Bratz dolls, which are marketed at young girls, wear make-up and sexually provocative clothing. Even children's stationery was sold on our high street bearing the Playboy bunny emblem, and a major supermarket was forced to remove pole-dancing kits from their toy section after complaints from the public.

Adult dressing

Photographs of various young children from celebrities' families wearing adult clothes and make-up have featured in magazines and newspapers recently. In our star-struck culture, celebrities' activities are avidly followed and imitated by many. A popular department store said that people's interest in celebrity children had influenced buying patterns in children's clothing. Many parents surveyed by the store said that fashion was as important as functionality when they were buying clothes for girls (*Daily Mail*, 2010). Celebrity children have been encouraging a trend for young girls to wear age-inappropriate clothes or items that over-emphasise their sexuality. It is not unusual to see children coming to primary school with dyed hair and wearing make-up, and young girls struggling to run in high-heeled shoes in the playground. In our high streets, it has been possible to buy high-heeled shoes in child sizes, sexy cut-off crop-tops, thongs, padded bras and bikini tops, lacy underwear and T-shirts with provocative messages for our young children. The NSPCC comments that by normalising sexualised clothing, young girls are put at risk of being exploited. They are unlikely to be aware of the messages that wearing this quasi-adult clothing may be giving out. Being dressed in this way puts undue and inappropriate emphasis on a girl's appearance and on looking grown-up, 'hot' or trendy at the expense of other aspects of her childhood identity.

Disability

The image of perfection that we see in the media can be very excluding for children with disabilities. Many disabled people complain about their invisibility, or total lack of representation in the media. If they do feature, the emphasis tends to be on their disability and how they have 'beaten the odds', or they will be portrayed as helpless and needing protection. There is a need for the media to represent the 770, 000 disabled children in the UK. Not only do they need this visibility so that they can feel less isolated and more a part of everyday life, but also their presence in the media shapes the attitudes of all children. Films, television and magazine images should aim to present disabled people as part of society's general background, or if the storyline focuses on them, it should emphasise themes other than their disability. Children's toys, books and television are beginning to be more inclusive, but there is a long way to go.

Peer pressure

Peer pressure to lose weight and peers teasing or making negative comments about a child's weight has been strongly linked with disordered eating. A child being bullied or teased by peers at the pre-teen stage, when their body is beginning to undergo so many changes, has a particularly negative impact on body image. Evidence shows that overweight children, primarily girls, are bullied and teased about their appearance more than other children (Lunde, 2009). The girls with the most unhealthy body images said that their peer group and parents frequently made negative comments about their weight or appearance. Children are influential carriers of society's stereotypes. Schools are ideally placed to help pupils not only to explore the messages they receive about weight and appearance, but also to have a sensitive awareness of the effect that their own comments might have on others.

Schools can also give children the opportunities and encouragement to support each other to feel good about themselves and resist pressures about the way they should look. In the 2009 Girlguiding UK survey, children said that constructive and positive emotional support from family and friends had enormous influence on their ability to cope with the external pressures about their appearance. They reported that this type of support was really effective in mitigating any damaging emotions or thoughts they might have.

This body image curriculum aims to help children to develop the emotional resilience to withstand pressures, and feel positive about themselves and their bodies.

3

The role of parents and carers

I'm always on diets, but I was really shocked the other day when my nine-year-old said that she should go on one too.

Karen, mother of two daughters

Children will develop the majority of their beliefs, attitudes and behaviours from the important adults in their lives. Despite the powerful influence of the media on body image, parents and carers are the main role models for their children. Although society's ideals of beauty and body shape can create unreal expectations, the influence of home is a crucial factor in the development of a child's healthy attitude towards their own body. Parents and family members have the highest impact on children's body image, and this is particularly evident for girls. Many of the most significant messages that children receive about their own self-worth and body image will come from what they see and hear around them in their families. The adults' own attitudes to food and diet, their own eating patterns, body image concerns and behaviours are highly likely to be communicated to their children (Phares *et al.*, 2004).

Ideas, values and beliefs about body shape and physical appearance are passed from parents to their children in a number of ways. They can be communicated through direct remarks or teasing about their child's appearance. They are also passed on more indirectly where the child picks up and models the adults' behaviour and attitudes. Many parents struggle with their own difficulties around body image and eating. A mother's own level of body satisfaction will affect her child's developing body image. Studies show that a mother's desire to become thinner can have a direct impact on her child's attitude. Studies by Harvard Medical School and others report that mothers who over-emphasise their anxieties about body weight are highly likely to pass those concerns on to their children (Field *et al.*, 2005). Children who observe their mothers' pursuit of thinness and dieting often internalise these same goals; in other words, they identify strongly with these goals and make them their own.

A mother who is constantly on a diet, does not sit down to eat with the family, prepares special restrictive meals for herself, over-exercises to lose weight or criticises her own body will be indirectly passing these weight and body image issues to her own children. One study showed that, by the age of 5, children were already feeling it is good to be thin and evaluated their own weight according to this ideal (Krahnstoever, Davison and Birch, 2002). Crucially, these children's weight concerns were not just influenced by their own perceptions about their bodies but also by their mothers' own weight concerns.

Young children have been found to be knowledgeable about the different ways to lose weight and most say they have learnt about these dieting methods from a member of their family (Abramovitz et al., 1998).

Of course, parents themselves are not immune from the media pressures to conform to the rigid, thin beauty ideal. As role models for their children, even the most healthy women typically experience anxieties about their bodies. Most women think that they are over-weight. Between 80 and 90 per cent over-estimate their body size, and at any one time, up to a quarter of women in Britain are dieting (Bryan, 2003; Croft, 2004). Although girls are more at risk of receiving and taking on negative messages about weight and dieting, parents need to be aware of the way their comments and behaviour can affect the developing body image of both boys and girls.

Parents' perceptions of their child's body and the importance they place on their child's looks have a highly significant impact on how the child feels about their own appearance. A child's body image encompasses their feelings about all aspects of how they look. Many children say they hate their hair, their teeth or their freckles. Parents should avoid talking about 'ugly' body parts or being too negative or critical about any of their own or their children's features. Direct comments or teasing about a child's appearance can have a dramatic effect on how children feel about their bodies. Many adolescents who suffer from eating disorders say that they remember, when they were younger, being upset by remarks or teasing about their appearance. For some, this was the beginning of their body image disturbance and eating problems. There is a direct relationship between negative remarks by peers and families and children's body dissatisfaction (Lunde, 2009). Parents must ensure that they do not over-emphasise the importance of physical appearance and attributes, and need to avoid making critical or negative remarks about a child's looks or weight. Research shows that girls receive far more messages from their families than do boys about their appearance (Phares *et al.*, 2004; Lunde *et al.*, 2009).

Warning signs that a child has developed a poor body image and low self-esteem may be a reluctance to take part in activities that involve undressing with others, such as PE or swimming, withdrawing from social activities and being unwilling to try anything new. Also, parents should be concerned if their child talks continually about themselves and their looks in a critical or negative way.

Parents who have positive attitudes towards their own bodies, who prepare nutritious family meals and sit down to eat with their children will be helping them to develop healthy beliefs about weight and eating. They should try to avoid labelling foods as 'good' or 'bad', but instead stress moderation, balance and variety. Families who are active together and treat exercise as fun and for fitness, rather than a way to lose weight, will be helping their children develop healthy ways to look after their bodies.

Children's limited life experience and their level of intellectual development mean that the messages they receive about appearance are very powerful. Children often do not have the understanding or confidence to disregard the constant media pressure they receive to achieve a particular look. Parents can encourage their children, through their own example, to notice the relentless media pressure to look a certain way. The adults can begin discussions at home, whilst watching television with their children or looking through magazines, about the images they see all around them and the messages these convey about physical attractiveness. They need to foster a questioning, challenging approach to society's rigid ideals of thinness and beauty. Through example, they can show children how to question and criticise the media images that are presented. This will moderate the effect of media pressure and help their children to become more critically aware of the messages they receive.

Whilst there is growing concern about the sexualisation of children and pressure on companies to be responsible about their products, it is the parents as consumers who need to ensure that their children's clothes and toys are age-appropriate. Clothes and toys that represent rigid, stereotyped gender roles and those that carry suggestive sexual slogans are age-inappropriate and need to be vetted by parents.

Although most parents would say they know what their children are watching on television, many would not be as confident about the content of their children's video games or social networking sites. They need to check the suitability of video games, ensure that they have filters on the computer and discuss with their children how they are using the internet. Children not only receive constant messages about slimness and beauty through videos, television, adverts and games, but they also see numerous hypersexualised images of male and female bodies. A recent government report said the parental role was to challenge and discuss these messages in order to provide an effective 'filtering mechanism' for their children (Papadopoulos, 2010). They need to be open in discussing sexuality in the context of relationships to help moderate the impact of the countless sexualised messages in our society.

Children need to develop a healthy self-esteem and feel good about themselves through their aptitudes and achievements rather than because of their appearance. Parents have a crucial role in making sure that their children are valued for their abilities, characteristics and values. It is important that children's fears and worries are taken seriously and that they feel heard. They should be encouraged to set goals and targets and talk about their aims, hopes and ambitions. Parents who actively encourage opinions, discussions and expressions of individuality will help their children to develop self-confidence, and feel valued and worthwhile. It is this inner feeling of worth that helps insulate children from anxiety about their looks and the need to conform to unrealistic ideals of physical attractiveness.

4

Introduction to the body image curriculum

Several mothers have expressed concern over their daughters' attitudes to their appearance. They're asking the school to help but we don't know the best way to approach it.

Richard, head teacher

A poor body image has serious implications for a child's social, emotional and physical wellbeing, so it is vital that we seek to address this concern in the primary school. Whilst schools have a crucial role to play in helping children develop a healthy body image, there has been very little practical advice and guidance available on how to approach this issue in the primary classroom.

Ofsted has recognised the link between emotional wellbeing and academic achievement. They look for evidence that schools are fulfilling their duty to meet the government's five Every Child Matters outcomes: being healthy, staying safe, enjoying and achieving, making a positive contribution, and achieving economic wellbeing. This body image curriculum contributes to these outcomes and builds on the work being done through SEAL (Social and Emotional Aspects of Learning), Healthy Schools and the PHSE curriculum. It encompasses emotional wellbeing and also explicitly reflects the modern reality of children's lives by equipping them with the tools to deal with the pressures that they face. It not only raises their awareness of constant media pressure, but also aims to develop their capacity to interpret and filter that information.

This body image curriculum uses a self-esteem approach to promote a positive body image in primary school pupils. Research shows that this is the most successful method to use when covering the topic of body image with children. In a self-esteem approach, there is a strong emphasis on celebrating everyone's unique qualities, talents and abilities. This curriculum is designed to enable pupils to feel proud and confident about who they are and to value their own and each other's individuality.

It also provides children with opportunities to critically examine media messages and to become more resilient to the relentless pressures to conform to a narrow ideal of physical attractiveness.

There is very little mention of diets or healthy eating in this body image curriculum. Research suggests that highlighting to children the concerns about weight, junk food or eating patterns can be counter-productive, particularly when covering a topic on body image (Pettigrew *et al.*, 2009). Obviously, schools need to get the balance right, and it is important to educate children about healthy diets, but it would be unhelpful to focus on this during a body image topic. It could have the unintended outcome of triggering anxieties about weight and eating disorders in vulnerable children. This curriculum focuses on celebrating everyone's unique qualities. It is hoped that messages like this, given when children are still in primary school, will give them the resilience to withstand the relentless media pressure on them to conform to a narrow beauty ideal. Children who are emotionally healthy, able to talk about their feelings and concerns and able to accept themselves on their own terms are in a stronger position to resist the pressures that they will inevitably face in their everyday lives.

Within this curriculum, some of the activities focus directly on physical appearance and other lessons help children to appreciate the importance of who they are 'on the inside'. The topic covers the pressures they might face to look a certain way. The children will be encouraged to think about how they might question or resist undue pressures from others about their appearance. It encourages pupils to begin to look with a critical eye at magazines, television and advertising. Throughout the activities, pupils are given the opportunity to explore and share their feelings, values and experiences. They will be encouraged to appreciate that their appearance is just one aspect of themselves and to value and build upon their many other strengths and attributes. As parents and carers are the main influence on a child's healthy body image, this book devotes a section to how schools can support, advise and help parents to approach this topic at home.

The body image curriculum is aimed at three main age ranges, although schools might choose to adapt the recommended ages to suit their particular needs. There are lesson plans for pupils at Key Stage 1, which begins the work on encouraging pupils to feel positive about their bodies. The topic is explored in more depth in Key Stage 2. There is a large group of lessons that have been designed for children in Year 5 because evidence shows us that this is the time when children are at significant risk of developing an unhealthy body image. There are further lessons for Year 6 pupils to reinforce the themes introduced in Year 5 and to prepare them for the challenges and changes that lie ahead.

The topic of body image is introduced through the character of a robot in Key Stage 1 and an alien in Key Stage 2. These visitors from outer space have been sent to Earth with the task of finding out about human beings, and so they have a series of questions to ask the children. Pupils are given the task of answering these questions using their own knowledge, insights and experiences.

It is envisaged that this body image curriculum will be used in its complete form as many of the themes build upon each other, but teachers can select individual activities and lesson plans if they wish. In each lesson the intended learning outcomes are clearly stated in order to aid planning. At the beginning of each theme the aims are set out clearly alongside the links with SEAL themes and the Every Child Matters outcomes.

5

Guidance for the classroom

I want to be sure that I introduce this topic in a sensitive way with my class.

Simon, Year 5 teacher

This body image curriculum has been designed as a structured, practical resource that aims to develop a healthy body image in primary school children. Lessons are grouped into three themes for Key Stage 1 pupils and are suitable for use by children in either Year 1 or 2. There is a larger set of lessons for Year 5 pupils, grouped into four themes, and there is a set of lessons grouped into a single theme for Year 6 children. As stated in the previous chapter, although the themes and lessons have been designed to build upon each other, it is possible to select and use single lessons or activities if required.

Each lesson plan includes the intended learning outcomes, a list of resources and, sometimes, additional ideas for extension activities. All the material may be photo-copied.

It is intended that at the beginning of each lesson the teacher presents a question posed by the robot or alien to the class. These questions, which are written at the top of each lesson plan, introduce the lesson topic to the children and also contribute to a plenary, when children can review their learning as they attempt to provide an answer for the robot or alien.

Advice for teaching staff on approaching sensitive issues in the classroom

This body image curriculum focuses on self-esteem and raising children's awareness of the influences that they are exposed to on a daily basis. The class are being encouraged to think about their qualities and skills, to recognise and celebrate the unique nature of human beings and, ultimately, to question how they see themselves and others and how that might be influenced by the world around them. In exploring these themes some children may say something that you are not sure how to respond to, or raise thoughts and feelings that you had not considered. It will help to read and consider the points below so that you will feel prepared for dealing with these issues if they arise in your classroom.

Informing parents

When approaching the issue of body image in the classroom it is important to inform parents and carers so that they understand the nature of the work and can support it at home. Chapter 3 outlines the vital role they play in their children's developing body image, and Chapter 9 gives practical advice and guidance to your school on how to include parents and carers in this topic. Encourage parents/carers to talk to their children about the themes raised in this body image curriculum. These discussions will support and reinforce the work that is being done in the classroom.

Support staff

If possible, it is recommended that you work closely with your support staff on this body image curriculum. Working alongside another adult can be highly effective when dealing with sensitive issues in the classroom. They provide another valuable perspective on the children's progress, understanding and emotional development. Include any teaching assistants or learning mentors in your planning and discuss the aims of this work together before you present it to the children. Be aware of the important influence adults have on children as role models for attitudes and feelings about appearance and self-worth. Ensure that all adults have a clear understanding of the reasons for using this self-esteem approach to promote a positive body image.

Classroom climate

To enable children to feel safe to discuss themselves and any potentially difficult feelings or worries, the classroom climate needs to be one where everybody feels confident to speak. You should be aiming for, and modelling, an open and honest atmosphere where people are able to voice their opinions, doubts or worries without fear of these being ridiculed or dismissed. You may want to spend some time working with your class before embarking on this body image curriculum, reminding them of their classroom rights, rules and responsibilities. Hopefully, your classroom rules will have been created together with your pupils and will emphasise the importance of respecting each other and valuing everyone's contribution.

In order to feel safe to learn, a child needs to feel accepted, supported and valued by all the adults in the classroom. Your children need to feel that you have warmth and respect for every individual in your class, and this project will be a good opportunity to assure them in this aspect.

Vulnerable children

When you work with your class on body image, ensure that your lesson preparation and delivery is sensitive to differing needs and perspectives. There may be children in your class whom you believe to be particularly vulnerable. These may include pupils with special needs, those on the Child Protection Register or children in local authority care. You may also have children in your class who are overweight or who you think may have issues with food or dieting. As this curriculum emphasises a person's inner qualities, and is designed to raise self-esteem, it is an appropriate topic for every child in your class. Any children who already suffer from a poor body image or who may be susceptible to bullying or teasing, will be helped by receiving support and compliments from their peers and realising that others have anxieties also. If you suspect that any child has abnormal eating patterns, it is important that you take this seriously. Offer them support and encouragement and help them to understand that you will need to discuss your concern with their family. They may need to contact their family doctor. There is a helpline for young children with eating disorders listed in the resources section on page 165.

You might wish to place a 'worry box' in your classroom throughout this topic, or perhaps permanently. This gives the children an opportunity to write down anything that is worrying them and to post it so that an adult is able to pick it up and deal with it privately with the child. Be aware of your school's policy on confidentiality and child protection and know who to go to if any concerns are raised.

Be aware of your own body image

Think carefully about your own attitudes and feelings about your body and your physical appearance before you run this body image curriculum in your class. You may want to do the quiz on page 163. As stated before, you need to be aware of your own influence on the class as a powerful role model. You may like to share a little of yourself with the class. Obviously, you need to judge what is appropriate, but you may have personal memories or observations that could aid a discussion.

Access support

If you are lucky enough to work in a school where there is a partner class for your year, you may choose to work in tandem with another member of staff. This will enable joint planning and sharing of resources. Build in joint reflection time so that you can both explore any issues that may have arisen in the lessons. You can also build upon each other's strengths and successes by working together to identify and develop positive outcomes.

Circle time sessions

Some of the lessons in this body image curriculum have been designed to run as circle time sessions. Most primary schools are now familiar with circle time; it is a group listening system where the class meet in a circle to discuss and consider issues together. It has a specific structure, which offers pace and variety, and the teacher aims to foster a democratic and inclusive atmosphere where everyone's contributions and feelings are valued. The adult aims to develop a facilitative role in circle time, enabling children to be reflective and to express and share their views and insights with confidence. To be effective, circle time needs to be fun and to engage the class, and should be a regular, timetabled part of school life.

Whilst these body image circle time sessions contain a variety of games and activities, they all follow the same structure. This provides a safe and predictable framework for the children to work within.

Adult role

The adult leading circle time needs to be empathic and non-judgemental and to value everyone's contributions. They have to keep in mind the needs of the group as a whole and each individual within it. They need to set the pace and direction to ensure that they guide the group effectively. This involves considering the children's needs for safety and belonging, and ensuring that circle time remains a positive and supportive experience for everyone. Where possible, it is extremely helpful to have two adults in a class circle time session. An additional adult acts as a powerful role model for pupils and can provide useful feedback to the leader on individuals and the group process.

Room arrangement

A circle of chairs provides an important boundary and structure and it is worth the effort of rearranging the classroom furniture to provide this.

Rules

It is important to remind the children of the rules at the beginning of each circle time session and to remember to praise the children regularly for keeping to them. Children may pass if they wish, as circle time is a democratic process, and they must feel that their participation in any discussion or activity is their own choice.

Name game

This introductory activity ensures that each individual in the circle has checked in and been acknowledged.

Silent statements

Children have the opportunity to state their agreement or feeling about something without having to put it into words. They cross the circle and change places if they agree with the sentence that the adult calls out. This is a silent activity and the adult makes no comment on the children's movements.

Partner work

Following the previous activity, the children will be seated in different places and will be required to work with the person next to them. As circle time progresses through-out the year, all children will have worked with a wide variety of their classmates. This develops everyone's social and co-operative skills and aids class cohesion.

Open discussion

Often the partner work will feed into this larger, whole-group discussion.

Game

Circle time games provide a useful way of including everybody, emphasising togeth-erness, encouraging equal participation and providing fun. Games also provide physical release for young children and give pace and variety to circle time sessions.

Sentence completion

It is important to use a 'talking object', which children pass round the circle to emphasise whose turn it is to speak. Completing a sentence round is a structured way of encouraging each child's reflection and contribution in a manner that retains some pace.

Ending

A simple whole-group activity, such as passing a smile or holding hands and passing a silent squeeze, provides a peaceful and cohesive ritual to close the session.

For more advice and ideas on running circle time, refer to Jenny Mosley's website: www.circle-time.co.uk

6

Key Stage 1:
body image curriculum

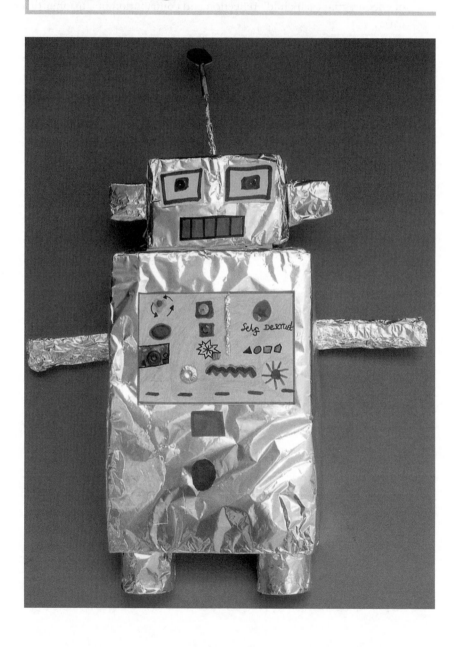

Key Stage 1

Theme 1

A robot arrives in our school

The body image curriculum is introduced to Key Stage 1 pupils through a robot character. The robot's task is to find out about human beings in order to report back to his home planet, so he poses questions for the children to answer. It is suggested that these lessons are taught in Year 2.

In this theme the children learn about the robot's arrival and make their own classroom robot. They are asked to think about the ways that people's physical appearance varies and what makes a person's identity. They are encouraged to reflect upon their own individuality and to feel positive about who they are.

Aims of this theme

- Introduce the robot character.
- Acknowledge the range and diversity in people's physical appearance.
- Increase awareness and appreciation of people's differences.
- Reflect upon pupils' own identity and what makes them unique.
- Enhance feelings of self-acceptance and appreciation.

A robot arrives in our school

Lesson links to ECM outcomes and SEAL themes

Lessons	Every Child Matters	SEAL
1. Introducing our robot	Enjoying and achieving	
2. Making our robot	Enjoying and achieving Making a positive contribution	Going for goals
3. The importance of being me	Being healthy Staying safe Enjoying and achieving Making a positive contribution	Relationships Good to be me
4. Why is the robot here?	Being healthy Staying safe Enjoying and achieving	Good to be me Relationships

Key Stage 1

Theme 1

A robot arrives in our school

Here I am. I'd like to get to know you

Lesson 1: Introducing our robot

Intended learning outcomes

Pupils can:

- work co-operatively in pairs;
- use information to make a design;
- identify the physical features of humans.

Resources

paper
pencils
crayons

Activities

- Introduce a story to the children in the following way:

Sometimes on a clear night if you look up at the stars, you can see one that is brighter than all the rest. You have to look slightly to the west of this bright star and you will see a planet called Zokkit. It's a very flat brownish-grey land. Instead of trees or plants, you would see metal towers and twisted silver wire and the occasional flashing light. On that planet there are no people at all; no children, no adults, no animals, just millions of metal things that we would call robots. They are like little computers that are extremely clever, but they are really different to human beings.

How do you think they might look?

- Encourage the children to work in pairs to describe a character that bears little resemblance to a human being. Help them to consider how this metal, angular robot might look very different to a person and have few of the physical features we associate with humans.

- Ask the pairs to feedback from their discussions how the robot might look.

- Direct the children to work independently to draw their own robot design.

- Provide an opportunity for children to present their completed designs to the class, describing their robot and highlighting the differences between the robot and a person.

Key Stage 1

Theme 1

A robot arrives in our school

Lesson 2: Making our robot

How do you think I should look?

Intended learning outcomes

Pupils can:

- contribute their own ideas to plan a joint project;
- value and use the ideas of others;
- use drawings to make a 3-D model;
- work together in a group to produce a model.

Resources

junk, e.g. boxes of different shapes and sizes, yoghurt pots, tubes, buttons etc.
silver spray paint
foil
glue

Activities

- Set up an art table with all the materials necessary to make a class robot.
- Remind children of their robot designs and tell them that, together, they are going to make a class robot.
- Bring the class together to plan the art activity. Encourage the pooling of ideas and a joint discussion about how their robot should look.
- With the class, use the children's drawings and ideas to create a design for a class robot.
- Allow all the children in rotated groups to help create the robot using the boxes and assorted junk. Ensure that every pupil has contributed in some way to the making of the robot.
- Spray-paint the finished robot in metallic silver or cover it in foil (unless your class has different ideas for their robot's colour).

Key Stage 1

Theme 1

A robot arrives in our school

Lesson 3: The importance of being me

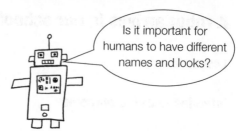

Is it important for humans to have different names and looks?

Intended learning outcomes

Pupils can:

- tell you why it matters to have a name;
- value their own individuality;
- feel proud of who they are.

Resources

large pieces of card for name-plaques
felt-tip pens
box and slips of paper for voting

Activities

- You should now have your class robot. Tell the children that on Zokkit the robots all look the same and none of them has a name. Help the children to think about the importance of having a name and looking different to other people, and imagine what it would be like if everybody looked the same and was nameless.

- The children work in pairs thinking of some of the implications of having no name and looking like everyone else. Ask them to consider the following:

  How would you make friends?

  How would you know who to play with at playtime?

  How would you get someone's attention?

  How would your family know you were you?

  Are there other things that might be difficult?

- Bring the class together to feed back the ideas and questions that came up in their paired work and encourage a class discussion. Ask the children to think about all the positive aspects of having a name and their own individual identity.

- Children design a name-plaque. They write their own name in large letters and decorate it using colour, patterns and shapes to represent who they are. These should be displayed in the classroom.

- During this lesson the children should have acknowledged some of the reasons why it is important to have a name. Suggest to them that it might be a good idea to name their class robot. They think about possible names. All suggestions can be put into a box and a voting system can be used to agree on a final name.

Key Stage 1

Theme 1

A robot arrives in our school

Tell me what humans look like

Lesson 4: Why is the robot here?

Intended learning outcomes

Pupils:

■ think about the range and diversity in people's physical appearance.

Resources

worksheet on p. 32

Activities

■ Ask the children what they can remember about their robot's home planet, Zokkit.

■ Tell the following story to explain his arrival in the classroom:

On the planet Zokkit, the robots love learning about new things. They know that there are lots of other planets and they have discovered that there is a planet called Earth, which looks really different to their own. They know that human beings live on Earth but they don't know anything about them. They are wondering what human beings look like, what they do and how they live.

They have sent one of their robots to Earth to find out all about people. They already knew that a school would be a good place to meet lots of people and that's why your robot is here.

Remember that on planet Zokkit every robot looks identical, so the first thing that he's noticed about people is how different they all look.

■ In groups, the children think about what their robot will have noticed about the wide range of people's looks and physical features. Encourage them to consider all the differences he may have spotted, e.g. heights, ages, colouring, hair type etc.

■ Ask the children what they think the robot will have noticed about people's different appearances. Tell them that he has to send a report back to Zokkit explaining what people look like on Earth. Can you help him to do this?

■ Children write a report using the worksheet (page 32).

Extension activity

■ Your class may like to make a paper chain of different-looking people holding hands to reflect the diversity of human beings. Each child is given one person to decorate.

→▲▲◢⚡◢ ↰◤ ⚡◺↳ △↑△↑△↳ △↓⇨⋯⇨←→→→↑▶↑⇨▽
↕△↑↓↓◢⚡◢ ↰◤ ⚡↑↓ △↑⋯⇨ ⋯⇨▶▶↕↘↰↔↓△△△
↓↰▽△◀ ↙↕

Report from Earth to Zokkit

Subject: Human beings – what do they look like?

Now that I have arrived on Earth, I have found a school and the humans here have given me a name.

I am now called ....

I have seen lots of humans already. Unlike us robots, each one of them looks different. I will describe the different ways they look and draw you some pictures...

Theme 2

Looking after ourselves

In this theme the children think about all the ways to keep their bodies healthy. They explore why people wear clothes and reflect on their own and others' physical appearance and how it changes from babyhood to adulthood. They focus on their own skills in caring for their bodies and are also encouraged to consider how they might help others both at home and at school.

Aims of this theme

- Help pupils understand what a healthy body is.
- Increase pupils' awareness of how they have developed and changed since babyhood.
- Increase pupils' feelings of confidence and competence in their self-care and skills of helping others.
- Encourage pupils' positive reflection on their physical appearance, identifying changes, likenesses and attributes.
- Enhance self-esteem by providing opportunity for pupils to offer each other mutual support and acknowledgement.

Key Stage 1

Theme 2

Looking after ourselves

Lesson links to ECM outcomes and SEAL themes

Lessons	Every Child Matters	SEAL
1. Keeping my body healthy	Being healthy Staying safe	Good to be me
2. Clothes	Being healthy Staying safe	Good to be me
3. How I look after myself	Enjoying and achieving Being healthy Staying safe	Good to be me Changes
4. Growing up and changing	Being healthy Staying safe	Good to be me Changes
5. How I care for others	Being healthy Staying safe Making a positive contribution	Relationships Getting on and falling out

Key Stage 1

Theme 2

Looking after ourselves

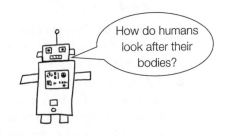

How do humans look after their bodies?

Lesson 1: Keeping my body healthy

Intended learning outcomes

Pupils:

- understand the meaning of the word 'healthy';
- know different ways to keep their bodies healthy;
- can design and create a poster to communicate information.

Resources

large poster-sized paper
felt-tip pens

Activities

- Write the word 'healthy' on the board and ask the children what it means. Share ideas about what we can all do to look after our bodies and ensure that we stay healthy. You could draw a mind map with the themes that the children suggest and ask further questions to elicit detailed responses. *Exercise* – why do we need to exercise our bodies? *Food* – what is healthy food and why is it important? *Keeping clean* – why do we need to wash ourselves? Why is it important to wash our hands before eating or after going to the toilet? *Sleep* – what happens when we sleep? Why do we need sleep, and why might babies and children need more sleep than adults? *Fresh air* – why is it good to breathe fresh air? Why do our bodies need it?

- How might we know if someone was healthy? It might not be obvious by looking at someone. Elicit from the children that a healthy person would have energy and feel alert.

- Help the children to consider what school can do to help children to be healthy (e.g. provide healthy snacks and dinners, give plenty of opportunities for exercise and fresh air, etc.).

- Tell the children that they will be designing an information poster about staying healthy. Remind them to think about all the different ways of looking after their bodies that they have discussed and think about how they could present this knowledge to other people on a poster using pictures and words. They may choose to create a poster illustrating just one aspect of staying healthy or they might prefer to include information on the many different ways we can look after our bodies.

- The finished posters could be displayed around the school.

Extension activities

- Discuss with the children who else might help our bodies to stay healthy. Ask them to think about the different professionals who look after our bodies such as doctors, nurses, dentists and opticians.

- Invite the school nurse, a dentist or other health professional to visit the class to talk about their role.

- Set up a doctor's surgery in the home corner. Encourage the children to talk about what people and equipment it would need and organise opening times, appointment times etc.

Key Stage 1

Looking after ourselves

Lesson 2: Clothes

Theme 2

Why do humans wear clothes?

Intended learning outcomes

Pupils:

- can name and spell different items of clothing;
- know reasons why people might wear different types of clothing;
- can design an outfit that is suited to a particular purpose.

Resources

body outline sheets
situation cards

Activities

- Ask the children why people wear clothes (to keep warm, to show belonging to a team/religion/school, to look special, for exercise, for hygiene, to protect the body).

- In pairs, the children name different types of clothes for different times and occasions and feedback to the class (e.g. sports clothes, uniforms, swimming costumes).

- The children think in more detail about uniforms. Are they a good idea? Why do we have them? Which types of jobs have a uniform? Why might this be?

- Encourage the children to think about clothes they might wear for different types of weather and occasions (clothes for holidays, parties, exercise, winter etc.). How might the styles and materials vary according to the season or activity?

- Children can also consider clothes from different cultures and climates.

- Play 'hangman' on the board with items of clothing. Draw a washing-line across the board and a big basket at the bottom. A child thinks of an item of clothing (e.g. coat, trousers) and writes the appropriate amount of lines to represent the missing letters of the word on the board. Children take it in turns to guess the missing letters until the item is guessed. If the item is guessed before all the letters have been filled in, the child draws the item on the washing-line. If there have been four wrong attempts at guessing letters, the child draws a circle to represent a screwed-up item of clothing and places it in the washing basket. The class see how many different items of clothing they can collect on the washing-line and try to avoid any clothes being screwed up in the basket.

- Give each child an outline of a body. They are given a list of situations and they have to design an outfit for one of the occasions (situations could include, party, wedding, going to a theme park, playing football, climbing, skiing, going to school, snorkelling, disco, playing tennis, going to the beach).

- When they have designed and coloured their outfit they can write about it, including a physical description of how it looks (colour, style, material etc.) and explaining why it was suitable for the situation they chose.

Extension activity

- Ask parents or people in your local community to come into the class to show the children a traditional way of dressing in their culture, or their own national costume, or a uniform they might wear for work.

Key Stage 1

Theme 2

Looking after ourselves

Lesson 3: How I look after myself

How do young humans look after themselves?

Intended learning outcomes

Pupils can:

■ explain how they have developed their self-care skills since babyhood;

■ name some of the ways that they are able to care for their bodies;

■ write detailed step-by-step instructions.

Resources

photograph of a baby
photograph of a child aged approx. 6 or 7
writing paper
pens

Activities

■ Show the photograph of the baby and ask the class to think of all the things that need to be done to look after a baby, e.g. washing, feeding, dressing, taking for a walk, nappy changing, cuddling, playing.

■ Look at the photograph of the older child. Think again about what we have to do to help babies look after their bodies and consider which of those things this older child will now be able to do for him/herself.

■ Place signs around the room:

I can do it by myself.
I'm learning to do it by myself.
Someone else does it for me.

Read out the following sentences and the children go to stand by the sign that is most appropriate:

wash my hair	*brush my hair*
cut my hair	*tie my shoelaces*
clean my teeth	*make my lunch*
feed myself	*cook my tea*
wash my clothes	*go to bed*
get dressed	*have an injection*
have a bath	*read stories*
cut up my food	

- Children choose one thing that they do to look after themselves, perhaps from the list above, and write step-by-step instructions on how to do it. They can illustrate each written step. Encourage children to include every detail so that someone else would be able to follow it.

Extension activity

- Invite a mother and baby into the classroom. Children can find out about the baby's care and perhaps watch him or her being fed or bathed.

Key Stage 1

Theme 2

Looking after ourselves

Lesson 4: Growing up and changing

Intended learning outcomes

Pupils:

- understand that we all grow and change at different rates;
- can place a list of developmental milestones in chronological order;
- can identify an aspect of their physical appearance that they like;
- understand that there are often family resemblances in the way people look;
- can use their imagination to draw and write about themselves in the future.

Resources

worksheet with developmental milestones
photographs of school staff when they were children
photographs of the class as babies

Activities

- Adults in the school bring in photographs of themselves as children. These are displayed, and there is a competition to link the right adult to the photo.

- Adults talk to the children about how they have changed since being a child and pick one thing they like about their appearance both then and now. They could also discuss who they look like and (if appropriate) if their own children look like them.

- Children bring in a photograph of themselves as a baby to display in the classroom. They also play a guessing game to identify each other as babies.

- The children discuss all the physical changes that have taken place and are encouraged to reflect on an aspect of their appearance that they like now that they are older. They also talk about any family likenesses and who, if anybody, they take after in the family.

- The children are given a set of cards, each naming a physical development milestone from babyhood to childhood (see resource sheet, p. 42).

- In pairs/small groups, the children put these cards in chronological order.

- Encourage a class discussion highlighting the fact that we are all different and reach milestones at different times.

- This discussion can be extended into a writing activity. Children can project into the future and write an imaginary description of themselves and what they like doing a few years from now, or even as an adult. They can illustrate it with a picture of themselves as they imagine they will look.

Physical development milestones

Photocopy on to card and cut out the squares.

Growing teeth	**Losing teeth**
Smiling	**Growing hair**
Walking	**Speaking**
Eating solid food	**Crawling**

Key Stage 1	Theme 2

Looking after ourselves

Lesson 5: Circle time session:
how I care for others

How do humans look after each other?

Intended learning outcomes

Pupils can:

- listen to each other;
- contribute to a group discussion;
- take turns and co-operate with each other;
- reflect on ways in which they can support others.

Resources

talking object

Activities

- This is a circle time activity. Refer to page 21 for a reminder of how to run these sessions effectively.
- *Rules for circle time:*

    Listen to each other
    Respect everyone
    You may pass if you wish.

- *Name game:* Children say their name and at the same time clap their name out in syllables, e.g. 'Hay-ley'. The circle responds by chanting and clapping together 'he-llo Hay-ley'.

- *Silent statements:* Ask children to cross the circle and change places if:

    they are wearing trousers
    they have some friends in this class
    they have had a drink today
    they like helping their friends
    they need help with things sometimes
    people are kind to them in this class
    they sometimes help do jobs at home.

- *Partner work:* In pairs, think about something you do to help others, either at home or school, and tell your partner. Feed back to the circle.

- *Open discussion:* Introduce the idea of caring for others and kindness. Ask children to think of things that they might do to help younger children. Is there any way that they could help somebody bigger or older than them? Ask if anyone can give specific examples of times when individuals in this class have done something kind for them. Kindness can include not only doing practical jobs for people but saying things to make each other feel good inside. Think about the importance of supporting each other and challenge the children to think of a kind act that they could do for someone in the class this week.

- *Game:* Children take it in turns to go into the centre of the circle and mime a caring or helping activity, the others have to guess what it is, e.g. feeding a baby, dusting, brushing a dog's coat, tying a shoelace for someone, setting the table. (It may be helpful to have a list and/or pictures of some helping activities so that children can select one to act out.)

- *Sentence completion:* 'I can help my friend by . . .'.

- *Ending:* Pass the smile.

Extension activities

- Start a kindness wall for display in the classroom. Children write on a coloured rectangular piece of paper (the 'brick') when somebody has been kind to them and add it to the wall. Aim to build a large wall of kindness that celebrates the warmth and support your children are able to offer to each other.

- Alternatively, children can make a kindness chain, writing the person and their kind act on a strip of paper and linking it to the last one. Aim to get a kindness chain stretching from one end of the room to the other.

- Have a kindness week. Encourage the children to think of ways they could help at home, perhaps by tidying their bedroom or helping with dusting or washing up. Perhaps they could surprise their parents/carers by offering to do something without being asked! The wall-building activity could be extended to home. Each child takes a paper brick home and their family writes about an act of kindness their child has undertaken. The child brings it back to school to make up part of the class wall.

Key Stage 1　　　　　　　**Theme 2**

Looking after ourselves

What do humans do to relax their bodies?

Lesson 6: Yoga and relaxation

Intended learning outcomes

Pupils:

- know how their body feels when they are relaxed and calm;
- have experienced some yoga poses;
- can use breathing techniques to calm themselves;
- can join in a visualisation exercise.

Resources

none needed

Activities

- Ask the children what they do to help their bodies relax – share ideas.
- Tell the class they are going to practice one way of relaxing their bodies.
- The class should wear loose, comfortable clothing and have bare feet.
- Tell the children that you are going to give them instructions for yoga poses, and afterwards they will rest together. Explain that yoga is a way of stretching and relaxing your body. Tell children to breathe slowly during these poses.
- Read the following instructions to the class.

   Mountain pose: Stand straight and tall with your arms down by your sides. Your legs and feet should be pressed together and straight. Spread your fingers and toes and look straight ahead.

   Star pose: Stand straight and tall. Jump your legs and arms apart into a star shape. Stretch into your hands and feet keeping your legs and arms straight. Keep your back upright and look ahead. Imagine that you have a very bright shining light that is spreading strongly through your arms and legs, helping you to twinkle and shine high up in the sky. Breathe in and out slowly three times.

   Flower pose: As a class, sit in a large circle with your legs stretched out straight in front of you and pressed into the floor. Your backs are straight and firm. Together you are making an enormous flower. On the next breath in, stretch your arms up tall above your head with your arms straight and your palms facing each other. These are the petals opening out towards the Sun. Now, keeping your arms and backs straight, bend at the waist and stretch your hands down towards your toes as the petals close in for nighttime. Stay with your arms stretched out and breathe slowly. Take a breath in and lead with your arms as you unfold your body to sit back up straight again with your arms reaching up above your head. (Lead your class through two to five sequences of opening and closing their giant flower.)

Child's pose: Kneel down on the floor. Your bottom is sitting on your heels. Make sure it stays like this as you stretch your arms straight in front of you on the floor. Try to reach as far as you can along the floor, making your back and arms stretched out and long but all the time keep your body fixed down on your heels. Now bring your arms back alongside your body with the backs of your hands on the floor beside your feet. Your fingers can be gently curled. Every time you breathe in, feel how it makes your back feel bigger and wider as your body fills with air. Let all the breath out and take another deep breath in. Breathe in and out slowly three times.

Relaxation: Find a space on the floor and lie down straight with your arms by your sides and your legs hugged to your chest. Your palms are facing upwards towards the ceiling. Let one leg and then the other down to the ground and place them straight out in front of you. Imagine that you are up in the sky. You are light and floaty. You have risen up to the sky like a balloon and have been running and jumping in the clouds. You are tired from all this running and jumping and you have found a wonderful white fluffy soft cloud to lie on. You are sinking into its softness. Your arms feel light and relaxed as they lie down by your sides. Everywhere you can see is blue. The back of your head is resting on the cloud as though it is a soft pillow. You close your eyes and float along on this cloud. Everything is peaceful and quiet and you let yourself sink into the soft puffy whiteness of the cloud as you feel it carry you gently along. You stay very still... think about your breathing reaching every part of your body. The air up here in the sky is really fresh and clear. Every time you take a breath you can feel it spread through your body. Breathe it out strongly so that all the air is released and you can take another long deep breath in. Try this a few times. Now start to bring your thoughts back to being here in this room. Open your eyes when you are ready, turn to your side, get up slowly and sit in a cross-legged position. Stay still and quiet for a few moments and think about how you are feeling now.

■ Remind the children that in the relaxation exercise they were practising lots of slow breathing. Tell them that when we are excited, angry or upset, our breathing can become very fast. Trying to slow it down can sometimes be a helpful way for us to feel calmer at those times.

Key Stage 1

Theme 3

I am unique and special

In this theme the children explore their own and others' identities. They think about the way both they and others look. They are encouraged to be aware of people's physical differences and feel positive about their own appearance. They also explore and celebrate other similarities and differences between people that are not related to looks, such as how we feel and our characteristics and skills. In this way the children are helped to see the many aptitudes, qualities and abilities that make us who we are. They are encouraged to feel proud and confident about their own unique individuality.

Aims of this theme

- To develop awareness and appreciation of the wide range of similarities and differences between people.
- To enable pupils to learn more about their own identity and what makes them unique.
- To promote a positive feeling in pupils about how they look.
- To give pupils opportunity to support and value each other.
- To enhance self-esteem and encourage self-acceptance.

Key Stage 1　　　　**Theme 3**

I am unique and special

Lesson links to ECM outcomes and SEAL themes

Lessons	Every Child Matters	SEAL
1. Individual identity	Staying safe Being healthy	Good to be me Relationships
2. Portraits	Enjoy and achieve Being healthy	Good to be me
3. Exploring our similarities and differences	Being healthy Staying safe Making a positive contribution	Relationships Getting on and falling out
4. Likes and dislikes	Being healthy Staying safe	Good to be me Getting on and falling out
5. Celebrating being me	Being healthy Staying safe Enjoying and achieving	Good to be me Relationships
6. I am good at . . .	Staying safe Enjoying and achieving Being healthy	Going for goals Good to be me
7. Our feelings	Being healthy Staying safe Making a positive contribution	Relationships Getting on and falling out

Key Stage 1

Theme 3

I am unique and special

Lesson 1: Individual identity

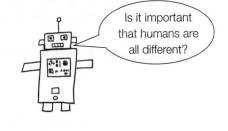

Is it important that humans are all different?

Intended learning outcomes

Pupils can:

- appreciate that we are all different;
- express aspects of their own identity;
- feel proud of who they are as individuals;
- make an individual contribution to a class art project.

Resources

photographs of famous people
squares of card
pencils, felt-tip pens, crayons

Activities

- A child sits with their back to the board. Show the class a picture of a famous person on the board. The class describe the person in the picture to the child with their back to the board. The child has to guess the identity of the person. Allow several children to have a turn using different pictures.

- Ask the children what information helped them to guess the identity of the person, e.g. job, character, appearance, age etc.

- The class creates a list of possible questions they could ask to find out about each other, e.g. favourite food, best day, what they like doing, who is in their family. Record these on the board.

- Children work in pairs. Choose some of the questions to find out about their partner.

- Each partner reveals to the class what they have learnt about the other.
- Each child is given a square of card and they decorate it to represent themselves using pictures and or words to show any important information they would like to share. They might like to display their age, favourite colours, animals, hobbies etc.
- The squares are joined together and displayed as a class 'blanket'.

Key Stage 1

Theme 3

I am unique and special

In what ways are human faces the same and different?

Lesson 2: Portraits

Intended learning outcomes

Pupils can:

- name most facial features;
- represent their face using oil pastels;
- appreciate their own unique facial appearance.

Resources

mirrors
art materials – oil pastels if possible
A5 paper

Activities

- Ask the children to name all the facial features that they can think of.
- Draw out all the vocabulary that you might need to describe a face e.g. colour and style of hair, eyelashes, eyebrows, freckles etc.
- Children work in pairs; they sit facing each other and describe their partner's hair and eye colouring.
- Give the children a mirror for them to look at their own face. Tell them that they will be drawing a detailed picture of their face and encourage them to notice features such as eyelashes, eyebrows, pupils, irises etc.
- Give children a piece of A5 paper and tell them to fill it with a large portrait of their face. Some of the children may need a template of a face shape to help them. Remind them to use the mirror for reference throughout this activity.

Extension activity

- Your school may like to give this art activity to pupils every other year as they progress through the years. If the pictures are saved by staff, they make a very good record of a child's development. The series of pictures for each child makes a wonderful display in Year 6 and could also be presented in a book as a souvenir for the child to take away when they leave the school.

Key Stage 1

Theme 3

I am unique and special

Lesson 3: Circle time session:
exploring our similarities and
differences

What do you like about the way you look?

Intended learning outcomes

Pupils can:

- listen to each other;
- contribute to a group discussion;
- take turns and co-operate with one another;
- appreciate the diversity in people's appearance;
- identify something they like about their own appearance.

Resources

large soft ball
talking object

Activities

- This is a circle time activity. Refer to page 21 for a reminder of how to run these sessions effectively.
- *Rules for circle time:*

    Listen to each other
    Respect each other
    You may pass if you wish.

- *Name game:* Ask the children to sit with their hands down towards the floor to catch a rolling ball. A child calls out their own name and the name of another child across the circle to whom they roll the ball. The receiving child says his/her own name and then sends it on in the same way. Ensure that each child has a turn and praise the children for including everyone.

- *Cross the circle:* Ask children to change places if they agree with the statement:

    I have curly hair
    I have brown hair
    I can swim
    I have blue eyes
    I have a fringe
    I wear glasses
    I have freckles

I like football
I have a missing tooth
I can ride a bike

- *Partner work:* In pairs, the children think of two things about their appearance that are the same and one thing that is different (e.g. we have both got brown eyes and a missing tooth; we have got different colour hair). Feed back to the circle.

- *Open discussion:* Ask the children what it would be like if everybody looked exactly the same and liked to do the same things. Encourage the children to appreciate how interesting it is to have such a wide variety of different children in the world and, on a smaller scale, in their own class.

- *Game:* One child goes out of the classroom and changes something minor about their appearance, e.g. they roll a sock down, take out a hair band, take off a jumper etc. They come back into the centre of the circle and the others guess what has changed.

- *Sentence completion:* The children complete the following sentence:

  'Something I like about the way I look is . . .'.

- *Ending:* Pass the smile.

I am unique and special

Is it important for humans to like different things?

Lesson 4: Likes and dislikes

Intended learning outcomes

Pupils:

■ can express their own opinion and listen to others;

■ appreciate the way that our tastes all differ;

■ are confident to identify their own likes and dislikes.

Resources

two round pieces of card – one with a happy face and one with a sad face

Activities

■ Place a smiley face on one side of the room and a sad face on the other. Explain to the children that there is an imaginary line between the two faces and that they must place themselves somewhere on the line.

■ The children will choose where they will stand according to how much they enjoy the activity; for example, if someone really liked football, they would opt to stand by the smiley face; if they quite liked it sometimes, they would choose to be in the middle; if they hated football, they would stand next to the sad face.

■ Read out the following activities:

swimming
playing football
watching TV
home learning
brussel sprouts
washing up
tidying your bedroom
computer games
dogs
riding your bike
dancing

■ Invite follow-up discussion:

Was there anything that everybody liked?
Were everybody's opinions the same?
Did you stand at different places on the line?
Would it be better if everyone enjoyed the same things?

- Put the children into groups and ask them to talk to each other to find out the following:

  Who likes the same TV programme as you?
  Who has the same favourite colour as you?
  Who has a favourite food that is different from yours?
  Who plays different games than you at playtime?

- The children make bar charts to record the class likes and dislikes.

Extension activity

- The class could do a larger survey of likes and dislikes in the school. They could think of questions they might ask other adults and classes and work out a way of recording this information. The children might like to ask their family some questions and identify some of their shared likes and dislikes.

Key Stage 1

Theme 3

I am unique and special

Lesson 5: Circle time session:
celebrating being me!

What do you like about being you?

Intended learning outcomes

Pupils:

- can listen to each other;
- can contribute to a group discussion;
- can take turns and co-operate with each other;
- know that who they are is not just based on looks;
- recognise that people have different strengths and abilities;
- feel good about their own qualities and talents.

Resources

talking object
ball of string

Activities

- This is a circle time activity. Refer to page 21 for a reminder of how to run these sessions effectively.

- *Rules for circle time:*

  Listen to each other
  Respect each other
  You may pass if you wish.

- *Name game:* Children introduce themselves with an action word by saying and doing the action, e.g. 'I'm jumping Jamie'; 'I'm hopping Zack'. The other children respond by copying the child's action as they reply, 'Hello jumping Jamie'; 'Hello hopping Zack', etc.

- *Cross the circle:* Ask children to change places if they agree with the statement:

  I am a fast runner
  I am good at making friends
  I like learning new games
  I am good at skipping
  I often play football
  I like painting
  I am good at tidying

> I think a lot about things
> I am kind to others
> I tell funny jokes
> I like cooking

- *Partner work:* The children have to think of things they are good at and share with their partner. They can try to find one thing in common that they are both good at. The pairs report this back to the circle.

- *Open discussion:* Acknowledge that we all not only look different on the outside but also have many differences inside too. We all like doing different things and have different qualities and talents. The children can think about some of their own interests and qualities and think about the particular characteristics they appreciate about other members of the class. Encourage the children to acknowledge not just the louder, more confident, members of the class but also how they might appreciate the child who always gets on with their work quietly, the one who is always reliable at tidy-up time, the one who never shouts out. These quieter children aid class cohesion and it can be very powerful to acknowledge their specific qualities. Ask the children to think about what it would be like if everyone was talented at the same things? What if we all shared the same characteristics? Is it a good thing that everyone is unique?

- *Sentence completion:* The children complete the following sentence:

    'Something I like about being me is . . .'.

- *Game:* Have a large ball of string, which all the children hold onto around the circle. Feed a small ring onto the string (a ring from a finger is ideal). The children feed this ring around the circle with their hands closed over the ring so that you can't see where it is or who is moving it along. The children have to pass the ring to each other in turn around the circle. There is a detective in the middle who has to try to work out where in the circle the ring is. The children make this job difficult by moving their hands along to look as though they have the ring. The child in the middle is allowed three guesses and then someone else takes a turn.

- *Ending:* Pass the smile.

Key Stage 1 **Theme 3**

I am unique and special

Lesson 6: I am good at . . .

What are our talents and skills?

Intended learning outcomes

Pupils:

- know more about themselves and each other;
- can tell you many of their own unique skills and talents;
- feel good about themselves;
- accept and value their own abilities and attributes.

Resources

resource sheets (pages 60–61)
glue
scissors
A4 card

Activities

- Discuss with the children the fact that everybody is good at something. We all have our own qualities and strengths.
- Acknowledge that sometimes it can be hard to remember all the things we are good at, but in this lesson we are going to think about all those things.
- Refer to the list on the resource sheet and discuss some of the skills that are mentioned on it. Ask the children to think about which ones apply to them. Perhaps they can think of additional skills that are not written there.

- Remind the children that this is a positive exercise. Too often in our culture we are quick to name the things that we are no good at or can't do but this is a chance to really think about our strengths. Ensure that, as children undertake this activity, they remain supportive of each other and respect the selection that each individual makes.

- Give each member of the class a photocopy of the resource sheet and ask them to put a small spot in the corner of every skill on the list that they think applies to them. Encourage the children to be generous with themselves; they can choose lots of qualities from the list. They must then cut these out. They may add their own words to the list if they wish.

- Give each child a piece of A4 card with the heading, 'I am good at ...', and ask them to stick on all the words they have cut out.

- Once they have finished gluing the words on, the children may decorate the piece of card in any way they wish, colouring or decorating the words or making a border round the edge of the paper. Display all the finished pieces of work in the classroom as a celebration of your talented class!

- Some children in your class may suffer from low self-esteem and could find it hard to identify their own skills. An adult needs to support them in this activity and name positive skills and attributes that they have noticed in the child. You may identify a group of individuals who could benefit from this level of support. An adult should work with this group, identifying their key strengths and encouraging a positive reflection of themselves and each other. Receiving recognition of their worth from an adult is an important first step in helping children to feel more positive about themselves.

Skipping	Swimming
Reading	Computer games
Making up stories	Washing up
Laughing at jokes	Lego-building
Being gentle	Being kind to animals
Looking after pets	Drawing
Helping people	Writing
Telling jokes	Tidying
Listening to stories	Helping younger children
Listening to my friends	Hopping
Climbing	Throwing a ball
Making things	Saying nursery rhymes

 Body Image in the Primary School, Routledge © Nicky Hutchinson and Chris Calland 2011

Being friendly	Being polite
Smiling	Joining in games
Riding a bike	Singing
Jigsaws	Making up games
Putting toys away	Choosing games to play
Dancing	Maths
Colouring	Tying shoelaces
Dressing up	Cooking
Catching a ball	Football
Sharing	Running
Jumping	Remembering things
Painting	Cutting out

Key Stage 1	Theme 3

I am unique and special

Lesson 7: Circle time session:
our feelings

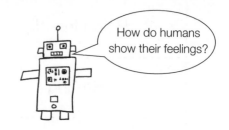

How do humans show their feelings?

Intended learning outcomes

Pupils can:

- listen to each other;
- contribute to a group discussion;
- take turns and co-operate with each other;
- recognise their own and others feelings;
- express their feelings.

Resources

talking object
music
tambourine

Activities

- This is a circle time activity. Refer to page 21 for a reminder of how to run these sessions effectively.
- *Rules for circle time:*

    Listen to each other
    Respect each other
    You may pass if you wish.

- *Name game:* Pass the handshake. The child turns to their right and says, 'Hello, I'm Sasha, how do you do Dylan?', and shakes Dylan's hand. Dylan turns to the child on his right and says, 'Hello, I'm Dylan, how do you do?' etc.

- *Silent statements:* Ask children to change places if:

    they are wearing laces in their shoes
    they have anything black on
    they walked to school this morning
    they usually feel happy at playtime
    they sometimes worry about friends
    they like pizza
    they have watched TV this morning.

- *Partner work:* In pairs, think about what makes you feel happy and feed back to the class.

- *Open discussion:* Encourage children to share their observations of their own and other people's feelings. Ask the children to think about a time when they were feeling very happy. What did they do? How did they look? Would anybody else be able to tell that they were happy by looking at them? Talk about how the way that we are feeling inside can show in our faces and our bodies, e.g. if someone was worried about something, they might walk slowly; perhaps they might be frowning slightly etc. If someone was angry, how might they stand?

- *Game:* The children walk around the middle of the circle with music playing. Stop the music and call out an emotion, e.g. 'frightened', and all the children have to freeze into statues that mime that emotion. Restart the music, then pause it and call out another feeling. Feelings to use in this game could include: excited, happy, worried, tired, proud, scared, bored, shy, thrilled, sad, surprised.

- *Sentence completion:* In a round, children complete the sentence:

    'Today I am feeling . . .'.

- *Ending:* Pass the smile.

Extension activities

- Find pictures of different facial expressions to use for further group discussions about feelings. The SEAL curriculum resources have an excellent range of photographs of children showing different emotions with associated discussion ideas.

- Have a feelings board in the classroom that displays a few pictures of faces showing different emotions. The children put their name by the emotion they are feeling when they enter school in the morning. They can change their name to a different feeling, as appropriate, at different times of the school day.

Key Stage 2:
body image curriculum

|

An alien arrives in our school

It is suggested that the body image curriculum is taught to Key Stage 2 pupils in Year 5. The lessons introduce an alien character to the class whose role is to ask the children a series of questions about the nature of human beings so that it can report back to its home planet.

The lessons in this theme help the children to consider the concept of beauty and how it has changed over time. There is an opportunity to explore the range and diversity of human physical appearance and the children can begin to question the importance placed on beauty and how little it tells us about the human condition.

The children are encouraged to define who they are so that they can explain human beings to the alien. They work together to consider all the aspects of being human and to clarify their own beliefs about the relative value of all of these.

Aims of this theme

- Introduce the alien character.
- Consider the concept of beauty.
- Increase awareness and appreciation of people's differences.
- Develop an understanding of all the aspects of being human.
- Know that a person's identity is not solely defined by their physical appearance.

An alien arrives in our school

Lesson links to ECM outcomes and SEAL themes

Lessons	Every Child Matters	SEAL
1. An alien comes to Earth	Enjoying and achieving	
2. An alien beauty pageant	Enjoying and achieving Making a positive contribution	Good to be me
3a. Finding out about humans	Enjoying and achieving Making a positive contribution Being healthy	Relationships Good to be me
3b. Finding out about humans	Enjoying and achieving Making a positive contribution	Good to be me Relationships
4. Aspects of being human	Enjoying and achieving Making a positive contribution	Good to be me Relationships
5. Space capsules	Enjoying and achieving Making a positive contribution	Good to be me Relationships Going for goals

Key Stage 2

Theme 1

An alien arrives in our school

Here I am. I'd like to get to know you

Lesson 1: An alien comes to Earth

Intended learning outcomes

Pupils have:

- considered how an alien might look;
- understood why humans look the way they do;
- used their imagination to design an alien character;
- worked co-operatively in a group.

Resources

plain paper
pencils
coloured crayons

Activity

- Read the following opening of a story to the children:

  The night was clear. The moon over the trees cast long fingers of white light through the forest branches, but from far up in the stars another light came. At first there was a tiny pinprick of green, but as it neared the Earth, the shape could be seen more clearly.

  Hardly a sound broke the silence of the night as the spaceship hovered over the trees casting an emerald glow across the surrounding countryside. There was a soft thud as the craft landed in a clearing, and a moment later, a gentle hiss as an opening appeared in the side of the spaceship. There, in the doorway, was the figure of an alien . . .

- Ask the children to consider what the alien figure might look like. Emphasise that this alien may not have any human features in its appearance. Encourage them to be as imaginative as possible.

- The children work together in small groups to come up with ideas for the appearance of the alien.

- Class discussion to feed back some ideas from the children. Elicit why their aliens might look a certain way e.g. they need eyes all around their feet to be able to spot tiny predators, they could have blue skin for camouflage in their blue land etc. Highlight the contrast between the aliens and human beings and extend the discussion by helping the children to consider the practical reasons why humans look the way they do (long legs for walking, two eyes for peripheral vision, fingers to pick things up, cook, hunt etc.).

- Children design and draw their alien and write a short description of how they look and why they have developed in this way.

- Children present their designs to the class.

An alien arrives in our school

Lesson 2: An alien beauty pageant

Intended learning outcomes

Pupils:

- have considered the concept of beauty;
- understand that beauty has changed over time;
- have considered whether people should be judged only by appearance;
- have worked co-operatively in groups.

Resources

card
glue
coloured pencils
collage material
piece of elastic

Activities

- Remind the children about their alien descriptions.
- Class discussion about what might be considered attractive on the alien's home planet, e.g. very sharp teeth, two wobbly green noses with pink spots etc.
- The children work in pairs; they look at the drawings of their own aliens and think about what would be their most attractive features.
- Class discussion to feed back some ideas from the children.
- The children are put into small groups; they are given card, collage materials, felt-tip pens/paints, glue, elastic etc. and asked to create an alien mask.

- One member of each of the group 'models' their mask in an alien 'beauty pageant'. The rest of the class comment on the particular features that make the alien attractive on their home planet, e.g. this one has particularly nice stripy eyes; that one has a wonderful soft fuzzy nose, etc.

- Class consider whether a beauty pageant tells you enough information about the aliens. Use the following prompts to lead a discussion:

  Do we know about their characters?
  Do we know if they are friendly or dangerous?
  Should we judge them just on their appearance?

- Display the alien masks.

Extension activities

- Tell the children that our own ideas of beauty have changed over time, e.g. women in Elizabethan times believed that it was beautiful to have a chalk white face; men in Victorian times sported large moustaches.

- Some other cultures also have differing ideas of beauty. Show the children pictures of tribes who consider long necks or extended earlobes to be attractive.

- The children could do a research project about differing views on beauty. Help them to understand that the idea of beauty is not fixed.

Key Stage 2

Theme 1

An alien arrives in our school

Lesson 3a: Finding out about humans

Intended learning outcomes

Pupils:

■ understand the key aspects of being human;

■ have worked together co-operatively in groups;

■ have developed questions to use in an interview setting.

Resources

none needed

Activities

■ Explain to the children that their alien has come down to Earth to find out all about human beings. One of its tasks is to interview a human and find out all about it so that a report can be sent back to its home planet.

■ Ask the children what information they think the alien will need to find out. The children work in pairs to share ideas.

■ Feed back onto the board using a mind map framework. Elicit the following themes.

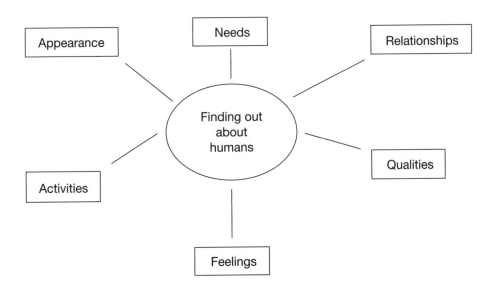

- The class work together to think about an example question to go under each heading.

- The children are put into five groups. Each group has one of the themes and thinks of four further questions for that heading.

- The class pool their ideas to create a comprehensive list of questions that the alien may want to ask a human. Tell the class that during their next lesson they will be role playing the interview and will need to think about how to answer these questions. As a class, focus on a couple of questions and consider how they might respond.

Key Stage 2

Theme 1

An alien arrives in our school

What are the important aspects about being a human?

Lesson 3b: Finding out about humans

Intended learning outcomes

Pupils:

- can work co-operatively in a pair;
- know different aspects of human beings;
- have had the opportunity to perform to the class.

Resources

list of alien questions from last lesson

Activities

- Remind the class of the work done on creating questions for an alien/human interview. Show them the class list of questions under the themes of: *appearance, qualities, needs, relationships, activities* and *feelings*.

- The children are put into pairs. They agree which of them will be the alien and which the human. As a pair, they choose a range of questions from the class list. Remind them to include at least one question from each of the themes.

- The pairs work together to plan their interview. Help the children to think about how they will start and finish their interview.

- Encourage the 'humans' to give full answers and the 'aliens' to ask supplementary questions when they can. The pairs may script their role play if they wish.

- Ask for volunteers who would like to perform their interview to the class. If possible, video the performance for future use.

- Ask the children the following questions:

    What was it like to be the person answering the questions?

    If you were really an alien, what would you think about human beings?

    Elicit the idea that humans are complex and interesting and that each one is unique.

- Children work together or as individuals to create a report to send back to the alien's home planet, outlining all the important information they have learnt about human beings.

Key Stage 2	Theme 1

An alien arrives in our school

Lesson 4: Aspects of being human

Intended learning outcomes

Pupils:

- know the key aspects of being a human;

- have worked co-operatively in groups;

- can reflect on the relative importance of aspects of being human;

- have been introduced to the theme of body image.

Resources

human aspect cards (resource sheet, p. 75)

Activities

- Review what the aliens have learnt about humans. Remind pupils of all the themes they covered when they were doing their interview.

- Explain that the alien is interested to know what people believe is the most important aspect of being a human.

- Split the class into small groups. Give each group a set of the six human aspect cards and ask them to work together to put them into a rank order from most to least important. Encourage them to debate within their groups and to create good arguments to persuade others why their particular ranking decisions are the right ones. Encourage discussion and negotiation.

- Class discussion to share ideas. Agree a class list through debate, reasoning and compromise. It may be agreed that some themes are as important as others and cannot be compared in that way. It is the process of the discussion that is of value here rather than the completed task. Ask the children key questions to help them think through the task:

    Could we survive as humans if we didn't have food and water?
    Are our feelings more important than what we look like?
    How would we manage without other people in our life?
    Would it matter if we all had the same qualities?
    Is what we do an important part of who we are?

- Ask the children to notice the position of the appearance category in comparison to the other themes.

- Tell the class that they will be doing some work on body image. This is how we see our own and others' appearance and how we feel about our looks. We will be thinking about whether other qualities are more important than how we look.

Appearance

Needs

Activities

Relationships

Qualities

Feelings

An alien arrives in our school

Could I take any objects to help the aliens understand what humans are like?

Lesson 5: Space capsules

Intended learning outcomes

Pupils:

- understand how an object can symbolise an aspect of human life;
- have worked co-operatively in groups to share ideas;
- can negotiate to reach an agreement;
- have had the opportunity to present to the class.

Resources

cardboard boxes
art materials

Activities

- Tell the children that the alien is going to take back a space capsule to its home planet. Show the class a box (about the size of a shoe box) and explain that this will be the space capsule and it will contain lots of important items that show aspects of human life to the aliens.

- In small groups, the children share ideas of what they would like to put in their box and why. Remind the class about the size of the box and the limitations of what will fit inside. Help the groups by putting the previous theme prompts on the board:

| Activities | Appearance | Qualities |
| Relationships | Needs | Feelings |

- Feedback ideas from each group and discuss as a class.

- Give each group a shoebox to decorate and ask them to bring items in from home to complete the space capsule.

- Ask the children to present the capsules to the class justifying their choices and answering any questions.

Extension activity

- The class could plan and make a space capsule that might represent aliens. Encourage the children to consider what weird and wonderful objects they would find inside and what that might teach them about the aliens' character, appearance and lifestyle.

Key Stage 2

Theme 2

I am unique and special

These lessons focus on recognising the children's individual qualities, skills and identities. They are aimed at raising self-esteem and allow the children to celebrate their strengths as individuals.

The children explore their own feelings about their physical appearance. Each child is encouraged to consider why they look the way they do and to recognise the links to their family of origin.

This theme helps the children to understand the importance of celebrating who they are on the inside rather than focusing on what they look like. The lessons allow the children opportunities to share each others' positive qualities and strengths as well as giving them the chance to develop strategies to encourage and support each other.

Aims of this theme

- Recognise and celebrate individual identity.
- Explore the concept of identity.
- Develop an understanding of how appearance is largely determined by genes.
- Encourage acceptance of their physical appearance.
- Share strategies to support others and develop self-belief.

I am unique and special

Lesson links to ECM outcomes and SEAL themes

Lessons	Every Child Matters	SEAL
1. The camera never lies	Staying safe Being healthy	Good to be me
2. Self-portraits	Being healthy Enjoying and achieving	Good to be me Going for goals Relationships
3. Who am I on the inside?	Being healthy Staying safe Enjoying and achieving Making a positive contribution	Good to be me Going for goals Changes
4. My identity box	Being healthy Staying safe Enjoying and achieving	Good to be me Relationships Changes
5. Who do you look like?	Staying safe Being healthy Enjoying and achieving	Relationships Good to be me
6. The diversity of human beings	Being healthy	Relationships Getting on and falling out
7. Talent show	Being healthy Making a positive contribution	Going for goals Relationships Good to be me

Key Stage 2

Theme 2

I am unique and special

Does a photograph show who somebody really is?

Lesson 1: The camera never lies

Intended learning outcomes

Pupils:

- understand that photographs can be misleading;
- know that photographs don't give us a true representation of the whole person;
- understand that many images they see in the media have been enhanced;
- can look at media images and advertising with a critical eye.

Resources

digital camera

two photographs of the teacher – one of which has been digitally changed in some way

colour photographs of each child on disc

computers with digital imaging capability that can apply special effects, colour etc. (e.g. *Paint box*)

YouTube ref: Dove evolution: a model's image is manipulated

Activities

- The alien who visited your class has now learnt a lot about human beings. Information has been sent back to its home planet showing the wide variety of people who live on Earth. Ask the children if photographs would be a really good way to show all the different types of people.

- Ask the children how often they take photographs or have them taken of themselves. Do they always look the same in each photograph?

  Class discussion exploring the idea that a photograph can show us in many different ways. Sometimes we like the pictures of ourselves and other times we don't. If we sent a photograph of ourselves to the alien's home planet on a day that we were feeling sad, then the picture would only show one aspect of us.

- Ask for one or more volunteers to come up to the front of the class. Tell the children that they can call out different emotions they want the volunteers to show, e.g. happy, silly, angry, sad, serious etc. Each time the volunteers change their expression, take a digital photograph. (These can be used for display or making emotion cards.) Discuss the idea that one photograph is only a snapshot of us for a moment in time; it does not show who we are.

- Show the class a picture of yourself. Ask the children if it is you. How do they know it is you, and is it a true representation?

- Now show the children the alternative picture of yourself that you have digitally altered. Is this also you? Can they tell what might have been changed? Tell the children how you have changed your image in some way and ask them to consider who else might use image manipulation with their photographs.

- Show a video clip that demonstrates how the media can change someone's appearance through manipulating a photograph.

- Show a glamorous photograph of a celebrity and help the children spot what might have been changed to make them look so flawless. Encourage a class discussion about the fact that the media changes pictures of celebrities in magazines. Ask the questions:

  Does it show us a true reflection of a celebrity?
  How might it make us feel to see the enhanced picture?
  What influence can it have when we see all these pictures?

- Allow the children to experiment with their own photographs on the computer. Ask them to create three different images of their faces to print out and display.

Key Stage 2

Theme 2

I am unique and special

Lesson 2: Self-portraits

Does a painting show who somebody really is?

Intended learning outcomes

Pupils:

- understand that a self-portrait conveys information about the artist;
- know that different styles of painting can present us with different information;
- are aware that it is possible to convey feelings and aspects of personality through a painting;
- have the opportunity to reflect on their own appearance and personality and present them through a self-portrait.

Resources

self-portraits from traditional images to pop art, e.g. Rembrandt, Picasso, Warhol, Matisse etc.
art materials – paint, crayons, pencil, pastels
paper to draw on and to use for collage
newspapers and magazines

Activities

- Ask the children what they think is meant by the term 'self-portrait'. Elicit the fact that these are paintings of the artist done *by* the artist.
- Show the children a number of traditional self-portraits such as Rembrandt and Van Gogh and ask what information they can glean about the artists from their portraits, e.g. what they look like, the sort of clothes they wore, the time they were living etc.
- Show the children some self-portraits that are less traditional, e.g. a Picasso or a Warhol, and ask them to consider what these portraits convey about the artist. Help the children to think about a portrait showing more than just physical features. Encourage them to look at the emotion conveyed through the pictures.
- Display *The Scream* by Edvard Munch. The children work in pairs to consider the following questions:

    What emotion do you think Munch is presenting?
    How does he do this?
    How does the artist use colour, light and shade to create the feeling?
    Look at the background. Is this important?
    What might the artist be saying about himself?
    What do you think about the painting?

- Class discussion to encourage ideas from the children. Extend the discussion by asking the children how the portrait might have been different if it was called *The Smile*.

- Tell the children they will be making their own self-portrait. Ask them to think about what they would want to convey through their pictures. Elicit ideas to create a list, e.g. interests, emotions, likes, dislikes, personality etc. Remind the class of the importance of use of colour, shade, expression, position etc. to help them plan their piece of work.

- The class works individually to design and create a self-portrait using a variety of art materials.

- Children present the portraits to the class explaining how the picture represents them.

Key Stage 2

Theme 2

I am unique and special

Lesson 3: Who am I on the inside?

I can see that humans look different. Are they different in other ways too?

Intended learning outcomes

Pupils:

- understand the value of people's qualities and characteristics;
- know that appearance doesn't provide them with enough information about a person;
- are aware that sometimes we hide how we really feel;
- can recognise their own qualities, characteristics, hopes, fears etc.;
- have reflected on their own individuality.

Resources

paper
scissors
coloured pens/pencils

Activities

- Ask the children what someone would know about you just by looking at you. Elicit a list of physical features such as height, approximate age, colour of eyes, hair etc.
- Tell the children that the outer appearance is just the wrapping paper – the real you (the 'present') is on the inside.
- In pairs, the children share all the characteristics that can be hidden on the inside. These may only be discovered when you really know a person or they might only be known by the person themselves, e.g. hopes, dreams, interests, memories, likes and dislikes, thoughts, feelings etc.
- Class discussion to share ideas.
- The children are given a folded piece of card; they draw a body on the card and cut it out so that when the card is unfolded there are two bodies holding hands.
- The outside can be decorated by drawing themselves and showing the outer appearance. The inside can be decorated with pictures, patterns and words to reflect what is on the inside.
- Children work individually to create their 'inside/outside' picture. These may be presented and displayed or kept private for each child.

Key Stage 2	Theme 2

I am unique and special

Lesson 4: Identity box

Intended Learning outcomes

Pupils:

- can recognise and celebrate their own individual identity;
- understand that objects, images and words can represent who they are;
- have worked co-operatively with others and shared information about themselves;
- have had the opportunity to present to the class.

Resources

shallow box
photographs
personal items brought in by each child

Activities

- Tell the children they are going to create an identity box to represent themselves as individuals (you may want to remind the class of the work done to make a space capsule for the alien that represented all human beings on page 76).
- Show the class an empty shoe box and explain that this will be the size of their identity box. Ask the class to work in pairs to think about what things they would want to put into their box that would express who they are as individuals. Encourage the children to include items that represent their likes, dislikes, hopes, experience, interests etc.
- Feed back ideas to the class.
- The class are asked to gather items over a week that they can bring into school so that they can make their identity box. Give examples of what the children might collect: photographs, stickers, old tickets, toys, pictures from magazines, souvenirs, badges, labels from favourite food, etc.
- The children decorate their box using photographs, words, patterns and colours that they believe represent themselves. They put in their collected items to complete the identity box.
- The children may like to do a small presentation to the class about their identity box.

Key Stage 2

Theme 2

I am unique and special

Lesson 5: Who do you look like?

Why does everyone look different?

Intended learning outcomes

Pupils:

- understand that their family genes dictate how they look;
- are aware of aspects of their appearance they can change and those that are fixed;
- can recognise and celebrate their personal family resemblances;
- have worked co-operatively in a group.

Resources

family photographs
YouTube ref: Michael Jackson face transformation (optional)

Activities

- Show a photograph of yourself with a member of your own family and encourage the class to guess who it is. Ask the children if they can see a family resemblance.

- The children work in pairs, talking about who they look like in their own families. It may not be their mothers or fathers but could be an uncle, aunt, grandmother or great grandfather. (Be aware that some children in your class may be adopted or in the care system. It is still possible to do this activity; many children have photographs of their birth mothers and fathers. However, you will need to be sensitive and check the situation before you begin.)

- Class discussion to feed back – highlight the fact that many of us take after a number of people in our family; for example, grandma's nose, dad's chin, mum's hair etc. and that some of us don't look similar to anyone in our immediate family but may take after someone in our history that we have never met.

  Help the children to understand that we are created by our parents and it is their genes that pass on to us. The way we look is programmed into us from birth, and although there are some things that we can change about our physical appearance, many aspects of the way we look cannot be changed.

- Split the class into two groups. One group considers all the aspects of our physical appearance that can't be changed, e.g. height, skin colour; the other group considers what we can easily change ourselves, e.g. hair, style of clothes.

- Feed back the two lists on to the board. Ask the class how it might feel if someone aspires to look like someone physically very different to themselves. Discuss as a class how important it is to accept who we are and be proud that we represent our families and our history.

- Ask the children to choose one aspect of their appearance that they hope they can pass on to their own children.

Note to teacher

Be aware that this discussion may well raise the issue of cosmetic surgery. Be prepared to talk to the children about the risks of cosmetic surgery, which is a significant invasive surgical procedure. (Help them to understand that this is about accepting yourself and being proud of who you are.)

You may want to show pictures or YouTube clips of some people who have had cosmetic surgery e.g. Michael Jackson, Joan Rivers etc. Ask the questions, Why do people try to change themselves physically? Do they look better? Does it make them happier?

Extension activities

- The children might want to create a simple family tree showing whom they take after.

- Ask the children to discuss this work with their parents and to bring in photographs from home showing the similarities between themselves and other family members.

Key Stage 2

Theme 2

I am unique and special

Lesson 6: The diversity of human beings

Are you glad that people look different to each other?

Intended learning outcomes

Pupils:

- have considered all the differences in human physical appearance;
- know a variety of adjectives to describe human beings;
- have worked together to create a collage representing human diversity.

Resources

magazines and newspapers (use a variety of magazines such as Sunday supplements, *National Geographic, Home and Garden* etc.)

Activities

- Elicit the parts of the body and facial features that make up a human being, e.g. one nose, two ears, two legs etc. Ask the children the question, If we all have more or less the same features and body parts, do we all look alike?
- The class discuss all the aspects of a human that can be different – height, hair style and colour, eye shape and colour, skin colouring etc.

- Split the class into teams and play a game where the children have to take it in turns to call out descriptive adjectives for different aspects of appearance.
- You should now have a comprehensive list of descriptive vocabulary that highlights the wide variety there is in people's physical appearance. Pose the question, What would it be like if we all looked the same? Allow the children to talk in pairs and feed back to the class.

- Class discussion considering the benefits of having such diversity.
- Tell the children they are going to design and make posters illustrating the wide range in humans' physical appearance.
- In pairs or small groups, children use magazines to cut out pictures of people and draw their own designs to create a diversity collage to display in the classroom.

Key Stage 2

I am unique and special

Lesson 7: Talent show

Intended learning outcomes

Pupils:

■ recognise their own special talents;

■ understand that they are unique;

■ have celebrated their own and others' skills;

■ have considered the fact that some of their skills have been inherited from their family of origin;

■ have performed for the class.

Resources

none needed

Activities

■ Ask the class to think about all their talents. In pairs, encourage the children to tell each other about activities they do outside school, interests or hobbies they may have, or particular party tricks they can do.

■ Feed back and create a list on the board.

■ Tell the children that people can sometimes do special things with their bodies because they have inherited skills from their parents. Ask if anyone in the class is double-jointed or can do the following:

> Curl their tongue
> Wriggle their ears
> Touch their nose with their tongue
> Raise one eyebrow.

■ Tell the children that the class is going to have a talent show.

■ Allow the children time to practice and encourage everyone to have a go. Anyone in the class who wants to demonstrate their skill in the talent show can perform for the class.

■ With permission, photograph or video the performers.

Extension activity

■ Ask the children to talk to people at home to discuss whether they share some of the same talents. These may be hereditary, such as tongue curling.

Key Stage 2   **Theme 3**

Looking after ourselves

These lessons encourage the children to recognise and celebrate what their bodies can do. They consider their own abilities and skills and are helped to acknowledge that everyone is good at something and that their skills are not fixed but can be developed and enhanced.

The children explore ways of looking after themselves physically and staying healthy. The lessons encourage them to think about health in terms of balance and moderation rather than size or shape. The children also explore how to look after themselves on the inside. They are helped to recognise and share their feelings, develop strategies to manage their emotions and practise ways to overcome stress.

Body image is introduced explicitly in this theme. The children explore their own feelings about their physical appearance, the importance of self-belief and the issues that can arise when they feel negative about how they look.

Aims of this theme

- Recognise and celebrate skills and abilities.
- Explore ways to maintain a healthy body.
- Understand emotions and develop strategies to manage feelings.
- Develop an understanding of the impact of a poor body image.
- Consider teasing and look at ways to overcome its impact.

Key Stage 2   **Theme 3**

Looking after ourselves

Lesson links to ECM outcomes and SEAL themes

Lessons	Every Child Matters	SEAL
1. Celebrating our active bodies	Enjoying and achieving Staying safe Making a positive contribution	Good to be me Going for goals
2. What we can do	Enjoying and achieving Staying safe Making a positive contribution	Good to be me Going for goals
3. Healthy bodies	Being healthy Staying safe Enjoying and achieving	Good to be me Going for goals
4. How to stay healthy	Making a positive contribution Being healthy Staying safe	Good to be me Changes Relationships
5. Body Image	Being healthy Staying safe	Good to be me Changes
6. My feelings are OK	Staying safe Being healthy	Relationships Getting on and falling out
7. How do I feel about my looks?	Staying safe Being healthy	Relationships Getting on and falling out Good to be me

Lessons	Every Child Matters	SEAL
8. Helping others to feel good about themselves	Being healthy Making a positive contribution Staying safe Enjoying and achieving	Relationships Getting on and falling out
9. Friendship	Being healthy Staying safe Enjoying and achieving	Getting on and falling out Relationships
10. Teasing	Staying safe Being healthy Making a positive contribution	Saying no to bullies Good to be me Relationships
11. Stress	Being healthy Staying safe	Changes
12. Yoga and relaxation	Being healthy Staying safe	Good to be me

Key Stage 2

Theme 3

Looking after ourselves

Lesson 1: Celebrating our active bodies

What can your bodies do?

Intended learning outcomes

Pupils:

■ have reflected on their own ability in different active skills;

■ understand that everyone has different skills;

■ know that their abilities are not fixed and can be developed through practice;

■ are aware that some people have particular disabilities to overcome.

Resources

two pieces of card, one marked 10, the other marked 0

Activities

■ Put up the number cards 0 and 10 at opposite ends of the classroom and tell the class that they need to imagine a line between the two. The line represents a scale of ability where 0 means terrible and 10 means fantastic. Check the children's understanding by asking what 5 would mean.

■ Ask the class to stand on the line at the appropriate number as you read out the following activities:

swimming	climbing
riding a bike	dancing
running	balancing
playing football	playing Wii games
skipping	hopping
catching a ball	

- Ask the class what they noticed about taking part in the activity. Elicit the fact that the children were moving up and down the line depending on the activity. Highlight the fact that everyone is good at some things but not everything; and that's OK.

- Ask the class where they would have put themselves for swimming six years ago. Remind the children that nobody is immediately skilled at an activity; we just need to practise and learn. All of us can move up and down the line.

- Raise the issue that some people have more difficulties to overcome to enable them to be good at something. Show a picture of a child in a wheelchair. Ask the children to work in pairs to imagine what it might be like for this child and what particular obstacles they may have to overcome.

- Show a video clip of the Para-Olympics and ask the class to consider the achievements of these athletes and the qualities they must have to enable them to achieve so highly. Elicit the idea that to be successful it is important to have a 'can do' attitude and determination to succeed.

- Ask the class to think of one aspect of their own life where they show determination and a positive attitude. Ask them to consider what that looks like. How would people know they had that attitude? What would they be doing and saying? Share ideas with the class.

Key Stage 2

Theme 3

Looking after ourselves

How do your bodies move?

Lesson 2: What our bodies can do

Intended learning outcomes

Pupils:

- have reflected on what their bodies can do;
- understand that they have different skills to others;
- have recognised the importance of keeping active;
- know how their bodies move.

Resources

PE equipment
digital camera
pictures of active people (use sports pages)
art materials – charcoal, pencils, sketching paper etc.

Activities

- Play 'Simon says' with the class, asking them to do a number of activities, e.g.:

  put their hands on their heads
  hop on one leg
  rub their tummy and pat their head
  dance
  star jump
  run on the spot.

- Tell the children that they are going to think about all the things their bodies can do. Put them in pairs and ask them to share what physical achievements they are most proud of, e.g. getting a swimming badge, achieving a belt in karate, swimming a length, riding a bike etc.

- Children feed back for their partners. Write the achievements on the board. Encourage the children to applaud the class achievements when the list has been completed.

- Set up an obstacle course or exercise trail around the playground or in the school hall. Allow the children to use the trail and take photographs of each other doing a range of different activities.

- Display the photographs in a montage showing 'our active class'.

Extension activities

- Show the children pictures, photographs and drawings of people doing a range of different sports and activities. Discuss the way the pictures represent movement.

- Ask the children to draw each other in active poses from photographs or life.

- Invite visitors to the class to teach the children some new activities, e.g. circus skills, drumming workshops etc. Encourage discussion about how the new skills were learnt and, if possible, perform for the school.

Key Stage 2

Theme 3

Looking after ourselves

How do you look after your bodies?

Lesson 3: Healthy bodies

Intended learning outcomes

Pupils:

- understand the importance of looking after their bodies;
- know all the different ways to look after their bodies;
- have considered the concept of balance and moderation;
- have worked co-operatively in a group setting.

Resources

none needed

Activities

- Tell the children to imagine that they have been given a fantastic brand new car. Ask the children to consider what they would do to keep their car in tip-top condition so that it looks its best and runs well. Share ideas on the board and include the following three points:
  1. keep it clean
  2. keep it topped up with the right fuel
  3. run it.
- Tell the children we need to think of our amazing body in the same way as a brand new car; we need to look after it in the best way we can. Ask the children what we can do to keep our bodies in the best condition. Share ideas.
- Write the following table on the board:

Keep it clean	Keep it working	Fill it with the right fuel

- Put the class into groups. Give each group a copy of the table and tell them to think about each column. What exactly would they need to do to keep their bodies clean, full of the right fuel and active? Ask the children to think of four or five ideas to put into each column.

- Feed back ideas as a class and make an extensive list on the board. Extend the discussion by introducing the concept of moderation. Ask the children to think about the impact of any extreme behaviour. What happens if I only eat salad? only eat junk food? Exercise all day? Explore the idea of balance with the class and help them to understand that moderation is the key.

- Give each group some time to plan a short presentation telling children how to look after their bodies. Encourage them to use mimes, role play etc. to make their presentation interesting, funny and original.

Key Stage 2	Theme 3

Looking after ourselves

What do younger humans need to know about looking after their bodies?

Lesson 4: How to stay healthy

Intended learning outcomes

Pupils have:

- understood the importance of looking after their body;
- considered how to offer appropriate advice to younger children;
- learnt that healthy people can be all sorts of shapes and sizes.

Resources

plain A4 paper
pens
coloured pencils
'healthy bodies' work

Activities

- Remind the class about the work done on keeping our bodies healthy. Tell the children that they will be making a leaflet to share ideas with younger children in the school to help them look after their bodies.

- Class discuss what they would need to include for younger children. Ask the class to think in pairs about what they would not want to put in the leaflet, and why.

- Feed back what was discussed, making sure that the children highlight the fact that size and shape are not the important issues. Stress the importance of accepting and celebrating who we are and what we look like. Remind them that balance and moderation is the important message.

- Put the children into small groups to plan a mind map about what would be in the leaflet. Encourage them to include all the information about exercise, food and hygiene.

- Groups share their ideas as a class and consider pictures, layout and key information.

- Each group creates a leaflet or poster to be used (if appropriate) with younger classes or in a school assembly.

Key Stage 2

Theme 3

Looking after ourselves

Lesson 5: What is body image?

Do humans mind how they feel?

Intended learning outcomes

Pupils:

- understand the concept of body image;
- know what might create a good and a poor body image;
- have developed strategies to support people who feel bad about themselves.

Resources

big paper
coloured pens
pencils
two pictures of the same person

Activities

- Write the words 'body image' on the board and ask the children in pairs, to consider what it might mean. Feed back.

- Tell the children that body image is what we believe and feel about how we look. It is not *how* we look but what we *believe* and *feel* about our appearance that creates our body image.

- Split the class in half. Show the children in one half of the room a picture of person (A). Tell them that this person has a very good body image and ask them to consider what might have helped this person to feel positive about how they look.

  Show the other half of the class person B. Tell them that person B has a very poor body image and ask them to consider why this person might feel so bad about their looks. Ensure that neither group sees the picture the other group is working with at this stage.

  Write some key questions on the board to inform their discussion. What messages might they have heard in their life? What experiences might they have had? What messages do they tell themselves? How might their idea about their looks affect other things they think about themselves?

- Feed back to the class from each group. Show them that both person A and person B actually look the same and elicit the idea that it doesn't matter what you look like; it's about confidence and self-esteem.

- Ask the children to imagine that person B is in their class. In pairs, discuss what they might do to help them feel better about themselves. Share ideas as a class.

Key Stage 2

Theme 3

Looking after ourselves

Lesson 6: My feelings are OK

What are feelings?

Intended learning outcomes

Pupils:

- understand the importance of their feelings;
- have developed their emotional vocabulary;
- know that all their emotions are legitimate.

Resources

emotion cards/photographs of faces showing particular emotions
big paper
coloured pens
pencils
positive/negative signs

Activities

- The children are put into pairs. Share out the emotion cards (see p. 103) so that each pair has a card. They do not show anybody else their card.
- The pair use mime or role play to show their emotion. The rest of the class guess which emotion is on the card. Build up a list of the emotion vocabulary on the board.

- Ask the children to consider the question, Why do we have emotions? Elicit: to express how we feel; to get help; to communicate something to others; to release stress etc.

- Place two signs on either side of the room. One has the word 'positive' the other 'negative'. Tell the class you want them to consider the emotion they have on their card and decide whether it is positive or negative. Then go and stand by the appropriate sign.

- Ask the children if it was difficult to do the exercise. Encourage a class discussion about the fact that it is not easy to categorise emotions as good or bad. Sometimes it can be positive to be angry, or we can be protected by feeling sad or worried. Use examples such as Martin Luther King or Nelson Mandela, who felt angry, and their strong emotions drove them to do good work.

- Tell the children that all their emotions are legitimate. It is how they deal with them that matters.

- Link up three pairs to make a group of six. Each group has two packs of emotions cards. They mix them up and put them face down on the table. Each player takes it in turns to lift up two cards. If they get a matching pair they keep it and tell the group when they have had that feeling.

Emotion cards

Happy	Sad
Excited	Scared
Worried	Nervous
Shy	Angry
Upset	Thrilled
Anxious	Enthusiastic

Key Stage 2

Theme 3

Looking after ourselves

Lesson 7: Circle time session:
how do I feel about my looks?

How do humans feel about their appearance?

Intended learning outcomes

Pupils can:

- listen to each other;
- contribute to a group discussion;
- take turns and co-operate with each other;
- understand the importance of being positive about themselves.

Resources

soft ball

Activities

- This is a circle time activity. Refer to page 21 for a reminder of how to run these sessions effectively.

- *Rules for circle time:*

    Listen to each other
    Respect each other
    You may pass if you wish.

- *Name game:* The children roll or throw the ball across the circle to another child. As they do so they say: 'My name is .... and I feel .... today. Make sure all the children have an opportunity to speak.

- *Cross the circle:* Read out the following statements. If the child agrees with the statement they stand up and change places with somebody else:

    I think how you look is very important.
    I value people because of their qualities and characteristics.
    There is no such thing as a normal person.
    I sometimes judge people based on how they look.
    People are all different shapes and sizes.
    I can think of one thing I like about the way I look.
    I can think of one thing that I don't like about the way I look.

- *Partner work:* Children work together in pairs to share one thing they like about the way they look. If there is anything they don't like about the way they look, how does that makes them feel?

Ask the children if there is anything from the discussion they would like to feed back into the circle.

- *Open discussion:* Encourage the children to discuss the experience of talking about how they look. Use the following questions as prompts:

  Which question was the hardest to answer?

  Why is it sometimes difficult to express what we like about ourselves and how we look?

  Where do we get our ideas from about what is attractive?

  Why is it important that we like the way we look?

- *Sentence completion:* The children take it in turns to complete the following sentence:

  'The thing I like best about my looks is . . .'.

- *Game:* Give each child around the circle the name of an item of clothing, e.g. trousers, skirt, socks, shorts and T-shirt. When you call out one of the items, those children swap places. If you call out 'wardrobe' everyone swaps places.

- *Ending:* Pass the smile.

Key Stage 2

Theme 3

Looking after ourselves

Lesson 8: Circle time session: helping others to feel good about themselves

How do you help others to feel good about themselves?

Intended learning outcomes

Pupils:

- can listen to each other;
- can contribute to a group discussion;
- can take turns and co-operate with each other;
- have considered the importance of friendship and what makes a good friend.

Resources

ball of string
small squares of card

Activities

- This is a circle time activity. Refer to page 21 for a reminder of how to run these sessions effectively.

- *Rules for circle time:*

  Listen to each other
  Respect each other
  You may pass if you wish.

- *Name game:* One child holds the end of the piece of string and throws the rest of the ball to a child across the circle. They say, 'Hello ...... great to see you today.' That person holds onto the string and throws the ball to someone else saying the same thing. Continue the activity until everyone has had a turn and there is a web of string in the middle of the circle representing the connections between each other. Can the class work backwards to untangle the string?

- *Cross the circle:* Read out the following statements. If the child agrees with the statement they stand up and change places with somebody else:

  I like playing football.
  I'm good at sport.
  I'm a good listener.
  I have a best friend.
  I like playtime.
  Sometimes I meet friends after school.

I enjoy reading.
I can tell a joke.
I've got a pet.

- *Partner work:* In pairs, children discuss what they think is important in terms of being a good friend. Feed back all the ideas to make a comprehensive list of qualities that they value. As the children come up with different qualities write each one down on a separate piece of card.

- *Open discussion:* The class discuss the qualities and characteristics that have been raised. The children debate and negotiate to agree which qualities they think are the most important. They place the cards in rank order in the centre of the circle.

- *Sentence completion:* The cards are then spread out in the circle and the children take it in turns to pick up a card and give it to another member of the class completing the following sentence:

  'I think [name] ... .is [quality] because...'.

- *Game:* Each child takes it in turns to instruct another child in the circle to swap places with them in a certain way (these might use alliteration but don't have to):

  'I want Jenny to jump across the circle'.
  'I want Sahid to skip across the circle'.
  'I want Zach to zig zag across the circle'.

Both children have to do the action while they swap places.
Continue the game until all the children have crossed the circle.

- *Ending:* Pass the smile.

Extension activity

- Guardian angels. Put all the names of the children on slips of paper in a box. The children take out another child's name. For the next week they will secretly be that child's 'guardian angel', going out of their way to be friendly, helpful and kind to that person.

Key Stage 2	Theme 3

Looking after ourselves

Lesson 9: Friendship

Intended learning outcomes

Pupils:

- have considered the importance of friendship;
- know the qualities of a good friend;
- have reflected on their own experience of friendship;
- have shared ideas to support someone who feels left out.

Resources

large paper
different coloured felt-tip pens
slips of paper with each child's name on
a hat or box

Activities

- Ask the class why people have friends.
- The class share all the benefits of having a good friend, e.g. someone to play with, someone who will listen to you, someone who you can talk to if you feel sad, someone to have fun with etc. Create a list on the board.

- Each child finds their partner by picking a name out of the hat.

- When the children have found their partner, ask them to talk to each other about a good friend that they have and a time when they have been a good friend to somebody else. This may be a personal exercise but children may want the opportunity to share with the class.

- Tell the class they are going to find out all about each others' friendships. Ask the class to think of questions they might want to ask and create a list, e.g. How did you meet your friend? Where do you see your friends? What do you like doing together? How do you keep in contact?

- Join up three pairs to make groups of six. They should be seated around a table on which you have placed a large piece of paper. Each child is given a different coloured felt tip. Ask the children to draw and decorate a small square in front of them on the edge of the paper about the size of a matchbox. This marks their 'home spot'.

- Nominate a child to start. They draw a line from their 'home spot' to someone else's in the group asking them one of the questions about friendship. That child answers the question and then draws another line from their home spot to someone else. Continue the activity until everyone has had a go and a range of questions have been asked.

- Each group takes it in turns to hold up their large sheet of paper, which should now be covered with a web of different coloured lines showing the connections between them as they communicated. They share some of the things they learnt from each other.

- Review with the children all the positive aspects of having a friend and ask them if they have ever been left out from friendships. Encourage the class to discuss how it feels when they are left out.

- In the same groups, ask the children to come up with some ideas that they could use for their own class to support anyone who ever feels that they don't have a friend.

Key Stage 2	Theme 3

Looking after ourselves

Lesson 10: Teasing

What happens if humans aren't kind about each other's appearance?

Intended learning outcomes

Pupils:

- understand the serious impact that teasing can have on a person's body image;
- have shared their own experiences of teasing;
- know some practical ways to deal with teasing.

Resources

none needed

Activities

- Play a game of 'hangman' with the word 'teasing'. Ask the class if they can tell you what it means.

- Ask the class to consider if teasing is ever OK. Encourage a class discussion about the fact that teasing can sometimes start in an innocent way, as friendly banter, but then can become too much and hurt people's feelings.

- Teasing often pinpoints an aspect of somebody's appearance and this can really impact on how a person feels about themselves. If someone is different in some way, this can be a focus for teasing.

- In pairs, ask the children to share their own experiences: Have they ever been teased in this way? What was the impact on them? Have they ever teased anyone else, picking on aspects of their physical appearance?

- Give an opportunity for children to feed back if they want to.

- Write the phrase: 'Sticks and stones can break my bones but words can never hurt me'. Ask the class to consider this saying – Is it true? Remind the children that teasing can have an impact on how we feel about ourselves and highlight the fact that saying 'I was only joking' is not an excuse.

- In small groups, ask the children to think about what they would do if they saw somebody being teased or if they were being teased themselves.

  What would they do?
  What would they say?
  Who would they tell?

- Feed back and agree a 'class charter' about how they think teasing should be dealt with.

Looking after ourselves

Lesson 11: Dealing with stress

Intended learning outcomes

Pupils:

- know what makes them feel stressed;
- understand the impact of stress;
- have considered ways to manage their own stress.

Resources

card
paper
pens
felt-tip pens

Activities

- Draw a picture of a bucket on the board. Tell the class to imagine that they all carry a bucket with them every day and that this bucket can be filled up with all the things in their life that make them feel stressed.

- Use yourself as an example and write up some things in your bucket that make you stressed, e.g. not enough sleep, children not listening, getting stuck in traffic etc.

- The class work in pairs and share all the things they would put in their own personal 'stress bucket' (they may draw/make their own buckets).

- Feed back some ideas and discuss as a class. Explore the idea that sometimes their bucket will be empty and other times it will be full. Ask the children to think about what happens when the bucket overflows. Encourage a class discussion using the following prompts:

    What does it look like when stress overflows?
    What would I see you doing?
    How does it feel?

- Draw a 'hole' in your bucket and tell the children that luckily it's possible to reduce stressful feelings, and tell them the strategies you use to help you feel calm, e.g. have a bath, talk to someone, go for a walk, deep breathing, listen to music, etc.

- Put the class into groups. Ask them to think of three or four ideas that they already use to help them calm down when they are stressed.

- Each group shares their ideas with the class and creates a list of strategies on the board. Ask the class what strategies the whole class can use to help each other and add these to the list.

Extension activity

- Make a 3-D bucket and put it near the door of the classroom. Put some strips of paper next to the bucket. Each morning the children can write any stresses on the paper and put it in the bucket when they come into class.

Key Stage 2　　　　**Theme 3**

Looking after ourselves

How do humans help their bodies to relax?

Lesson 12: Yoga and relaxation

Intended learning outcomes

Pupils:

- know how their body feels when they are relaxed and calm;
- have experienced some yoga poses;
- can use breathing techniques to calm themselves;
- can join in a visualisation exercise.

Resources

none needed

Activities

- Find out from the class what they already do to help their bodies relax.
- Tell the class they are going to practice one way of relaxing their bodies.
- The class should wear loose comfortable clothing and have bare feet.
- Tell the children that you are going to give them instructions for yoga poses, and afterwards they will rest together. Explain that yoga is a way of stretching and relaxing your body. Tell children to breathe slowly during these poses.
- Read the following instructions to the class:

Dog pose. Kneel on your hands and knees so that your shoulders are over your hands and your hips are over your knees. Tuck your toes under and straighten your legs as you lift your hips high up in the air. This is called 'dog pose'. You may have seen how a dog stretches out its legs after it has been resting. Imagine you have a big tail and you are trying to reach the ceiling with it. Look towards your toes and stretch your body back. Spread your hands wide like paws pressing into the ground.

Greet the sun. Stand upright with your feet and legs pressed together. Your legs are standing firm and straight. Your back and neck are stretching upwards. Your arms are hanging straight down by your side. Spread your toes and fingers apart. Your feet and legs are standing strong and firm on the floor. Stay still in this position and breathe in and out slowly three to five times. Now stretch your arms up and reach for the sky. Imagine you are trying to reach the sun. Now bend your legs a little and bring your arms down, keep them straight as though you're going to dive into the ground. Straighten your legs if you can and really bend from your waist, trying to reach your legs with your stomach. Let your hands touch the floor next to your feet. Stay like this for a couple of breaths. Now stretch upwards again to reach the sun, arms straight above your head and your body still and straight. Keep in this position for two breaths.

Tree pose. Stand straight and tall. Find a place straight ahead of you to look at and breathe steadily. Keep your left leg firm and straight and bend your right leg slowly. Place your right foot above the knee on the side of your left, standing leg. Make your left leg strong like the trunk of the tree. On the next breath in, stretch your arms up tall above your head like the branches, with your arms straight and your palms facing each other. Imagine that your branches are trying to stretch upwards strongly towards the sky, whilst the trunk stays firmly rooted to the ground. Take some slow even breaths and then slowly unfold your right leg. Place it on the floor and try the pose again with the other leg.

Relaxation

- Find a space on the floor and lie down straight with your arms by your sides, your legs slightly apart and your palms facing upwards towards the ceiling. Imagine that you have been running hard and you are very tired and you need to rest. You have found a quiet place under a large tree. If you look straight up you can see patches of blue sky between the leafy branches. You are pleased to be in this place because it is quiet and peaceful. You are lying very still and feel floppy and relaxed. Occasionally you can feel a gentle breeze and you can hear a faint rustling noise as it blows the leaves. You can close your eyes if you wish.

  Listen to your breathing and notice how it makes your body rise and fall, rise and fall. You can feel the cool grass touching the backs of your hands. One by one you curl your fingers on your right hand until you have made a tight fist. You squeeze it for a moment and then let it go limp. That feeling of floppiness travels all the way up your arm to your shoulder. Now do the same on your left hand, curl your fingers into a tight fist and let your fingers uncurl and relax. Feel that limpness travel all the way up your arm to your shoulder. Your neck is long and the back of your head is touching the soft grass. You can feel the grass on the backs of your legs. It feels soft and cool. Move your right foot in small circles, wiggle your toes and them let them lie still. Now move your left foot round in small circles, wiggling your toes, then let it flop down on the ground. Think about the cool grass underneath your whole body and lie still. Nothing moves. The air is fresh and cool and you take a long deep slow breath in and, then let it all out slowly and steadily before you inhale again. Try this a few times. Start to bring your thoughts back to being here in this room. Open your eyes when you are ready, turn to your side, get up slowly and sit in a cross-legged position. Stay still and quiet for a few moments and notice how you are feeling now.

Extension activities

- You can build relaxation exercises into your regular timetable with your class. It is beneficial to have time in the school day that is quieter and gives children the space to unwind and relax.

- There may be a qualified yoga teacher in your area who could offer regular yoga sessions to your class. Schools who provide yoga sessions for children say that they notice a marked improvement in their pupils' ability to cope with stress and stay calm and relaxed.

What influences us?

These lessons explore the range of images that children are exposed to and explicitly address how these might influence their body image. The children are made aware of how the media manipulate images and create celebrity-type lifestyles to suggest an idealised way of being.

The aim of these lessons is to raise critical awareness by encouraging the children to question media images and the messages they are given about how they should look and what girls and boys should be like.

There are specific lessons about peer pressure where the children have the opportunity to role play scenarios, explore the impact of their behaviour and consider alternative ways of behaving that support and encourage a positive body image.

Aims of the theme

- Develop an understanding of the meaning of influence.

- Raise awareness of the impact that television, magazines, adverts, peers and the internet can have on body image.

- Consider the influence of children's stories, toys and games on attitudes about gender and appearance.

- Encourage questioning and develop resilience to media and peer pressure about physical appearance.

- Realise how peer pressure can contribute to a poor self-image and have strategies to cope with these pressures and support others.

Key Stage 2

Theme 4

What influences us?

Lesson links to ECM outcomes and SEAL themes

Lessons	Every Child Matters	SEAL
1. Influences	Being healthy Staying safe	Good to be me Going for goals
2. Television	Enjoying and achieving Being healthy	Relationships
3. Advertising	Being healthy Making a positive contribution	Going for goals Good to be me
4. Peer pressure	Being healthy Staying safe Making a positive contribution	Getting on and falling out Relationships
5. Role models	Being healthy Staying safe Making a positive contribution	Relationships Going for goals
6. Fashion	Being healthy Staying safe	Good to be me Relationships Changes

Lessons	Every Child Matters	SEAL
7. Social networking	Being safe Being healthy	Relationships Getting on and falling out
8. Toys and games	Being healthy Being safe	Good to be me
9. Fairy tales	Being healthy Staying safe	Good to be me

Key Stage 2

Theme 4

Influences

> Humans look at images of people every day – does this affect you?

Lesson 1: Influences

Intended learning outcomes

Pupils have:

- considered the different influences they are exposed to;
- reflected on how much they are influenced by the media, peer groups and family;
- worked co-operatively to consider how they are influenced.

Resources

football hat, scarf, top etc. from the same team
headphones

Activities

- Make a request for two volunteers – a boy and a girl. Put the football hat on the boy and the scarf on the girl. Tell them that they are Mr and Mrs Smith and ask the class which football team they support. Ask for another volunteer; this is their son/daughter. Who do you think they will support? Ask the class why they think they will support the same team.

- Ask for another volunteer. Put headphones on them and tell the class that this girl/boy loves listening to [recent pop band]: Ask who else might listen to the same pop band? Elicit the idea that they can be influenced by other people in what they like or think.

- Ask the children to define the meaning of the word 'influence'. Help them to understand that it refers to the way that something or someone has power to have an effect on someone else.

- Tell the children that we are all influenced every day by people and things around us and that during this lesson they will be thinking generally about what or who influences them and has an effect on how they see themselves.

- Tell the children that we are all exposed to hundreds of images of people on a daily basis. Put them in pairs and ask them to think about where they see these images.

- Each pair feeds back to the whole class. Write the heading 'Influences' on the board and create a list from the children's comments including: characters from television and film, people in adverts, models on billboards, mobile phone photographs, celebrities in newspapers and magazines, singers, images through computer games and the internet etc.

- Ask the children what the majority of these people look like and if this is representative of real life. What message comes across by these images being presented to us all the time? How might these images impact on how we see ourselves? Does anything or anybody else influence the way we see ourselves?

- Encourage the class to think about the other influences and add further points to your board list including: family, friends, role models etc.

- Create a line across your classroom. One end is the most influence and the other represents the least influence. Ask the children to place themselves on the line according to how much power the influence has over them. Read out the following list while the children move up and down the line:

  television
  celebrities
  magazine pictures
  adverts
  Facebook and social networking
  computer images
  my friends
  my family
  role models.

- Ask the children what they noticed about doing that exercise:

  Did one influence have more power than any other?
  Did any influence have agreement from everybody?
  Were there any big differences between people?
  Were there any big differences between boys and girls?

- In pairs/small groups ask the children to share their own experiences. What is their biggest influence? Do they think the media effects them, and how? Have their family or friends had any influence. Do they think *they* have an influence on other people?

Extension activities

- Encourage the children to talk to their own families about this activity.

- Ask them to notice how many times they see images of glamorous people over the next few days.

Key Stage 2

Theme 4

Influences

Lesson 2: Television

Does television show what humans are really like?

Intended learning outcomes

Pupils:

- are aware of the amount of time they spend watching television;

- know that some television programmes could have an influence on how people see themselves;

- understand that some programmes may be delivering a message to the viewers;

- have worked co-operatively in groups to share ideas and opinions;

- have thought about ways to change and improve the way television presents some issues.

Resources

none needed

Activities

- Ask the children whether they watched television before school this morning and whether they will watch it again this evening. Get them to estimate how many hours of television they watch each day. Add up the time and write up a total of how many hours the class spends watching television each day. Ask the children if they think they spend too much time watching TV. Tell the children that this lesson is about how television might influence us.

- In pairs, the children share as many types of television programme that they can think of. Feed back and create a list on the board, include talent shows, reality TV, American comedy, soaps, cartoons, documentaries, news etc.

- Divide the class into four groups. Each group has one of the following categories: soaps, American comedies, makeover programmes and reality talent shows.

- Ask the groups to consider the following questions:

    What is the purpose of the programme?
    What do you like about this type of programme?
    What do you dislike and why?

Think about the main characters in these programmes. What do they look like and is their appearance important? What message do you think the programme is trying to give you? How could people be influenced by this programme?

- Each group presents back to the class what they have discussed. Encourage the children to think about how these programmes might have a positive or negative influence on viewers.

- Ask the children to write a letter to the producer of their television show outlining what they like about the programme, what they think might have a negative influence on people and how it could be improved.

Extension activity

- Encourage the children to discuss their work with their families at home and to look out for the images and messages that are presented to us through television.

| Key Stage 2 | Theme 4 |

Influences

Lesson 3: Advertising

> Do the images that humans see in adverts have an impact on them?

Intended learning outcomes

Pupils:

- know how adverts use images of people to sell products;
- can understand the impact of advertising;
- have created an advert that doesn't influence people in the same way;
- have had the opportunity to present to the class.

Resources

magazine adverts

Activities

- Choose a glamorous advert from a magazine and show it to the children. Ask them to describe what they see, what is being advertised, what the people in the advert look like and how they are selling the product.

- Ask the children to talk in pairs about what types of adverts they notice and where they see them. Feed back to the class – elicit billboards, television, cinema, internet, magazines etc.

- Put the class into small groups to look through a selection of adverts cut from magazines and have the following questions on the board for them to consider:

    What is the advert for?
    Who is it aimed at?
    How does the picture help?
    What does the model look like?
    How does it persuade you to buy the product?

- Feed back from the groups and encourage a class discussion about how realistic the images are. Remind the class about image manipulation (lesson 1, page 79) and highlight the pressure that people can feel to look like the images of the people in adverts.

- Give each group a type of product, such as soap, perfume, shampoo etc. Ask them to design an advert that is more realistic. Encourage the class to be funny and imaginative!

- Present the adverts to the class.

- As home learning, encourage the children to notice the use of images in advertising by looking at magazines, posters and television adverts with a critical eye.

Key Stage 2

Theme 4

Influences

Lesson 4: Peer pressure

How do your classmates influence how you feel about yourself?

Intended learning outcomes

Pupils:

- have considered the influence of peer groups;
- recognise how influential their peers can be on their self-image;
- have reflected on their own experience of peer influence;
- understand the emotional impact of peer pressure through role play scenarios;
- have considered how to develop positive peer relationships;
- have had the opportunity to work in a group and perform to the class.

Resources

drama scenarios (resource sheet, p. 127)
true/false cards
video recorder (optional)

Activities

- Ask the class what is meant by 'peer pressure'. Elicit the idea that it is the pressure to do or be the same as our friends or other children of our age.

- Each child has a true/false card. Read out the following statements and ask the children to hold up the appropriate card for them. Be clear that there is no right or wrong answer and that the aim of the activity is to help children think about their own feelings and attitudes.

   I like to wear similar clothes to my friends.
   I like to look different to my friends.
   I find it difficult to say something nice about the way I look.
   I often give compliments about the way somebody else looks.
   I find it hard to take a compliment.
   Sometimes I feel upset by other people making comments about me and my appearance.
   I worry whether friends will like my clothes.
   I like to look fashionable.
   I have made comments about other people's appearance that may have upset them.

- Allow the children to discuss some of the issues raised if they want to; however, make it clear that they can't name another child during that discussion but can talk about their own feelings.

- Split the class into groups. Give each group a drama scenario. The children will need time to develop the scenario and practise a short role play that they will be asked to perform to the class.

- Encourage each group to consider the feelings and thoughts of the people involved.

- Allow the children to perform their short role play encouraging the rest of the class to be a 'quality audience' and applaud their efforts. Then ask them to do it again – this time stop the action at different key moments to 'hot-seat' the characters in role or to question the audience: How are they feeling? How do you know? What might they say at this point? What would be a better response?

- Encourage a class discussion after each performance to reflect on the children's thoughts and feelings about what they have seen.

- Video the performances for future use.

Extension activity

- Write the drama scenario titles up on the board and elicit the emotions that have been generated by each one.

Drama scenarios	Feelings
The birthday party The nickname The swimming pool Non-uniform day	

- The children generate as many feeling words as possible. Notice how many negative emotions are written.

- As a class, consider the opposing positive feelings. Each group is then asked to re-enact the role plays to create a situation that would cause a more positive response.

- Use hot-seating and freeze-frame to help the children analyse how our actions have an impact on others.

Drama scenarios

The birthday party

Scene: a child's house

There is a birthday party. All the children are there having fun. A girl arrives wearing a new dress and it is exactly the same one that another party guest is wearing. Everyone says that the other girl looks much better in her new dress.

The nickname

Scene: the playground

Two children are good friends. One has given the other a nickname related to his or her appearance. It started as a joke but now the other children are using the nickname and s/he feels very unhappy about it.

The swimming pool

Scene: changing rooms

There is a swimming lesson at school. One pupil is changing and hears some of the class giggling and whispering. S/he thinks they might be talking and laughing about him/her.

Non-uniform day

Scene: the classroom

It is non-uniform day. One pupil is wearing trainers, which the other children make fun of. The pupil is very upset.

Influences

Lesson 5: Role models

Do humans look up to other people and want to be like them?

Intended learning outcomes

Pupils:

- understand the qualities of a role model;
- have identified their role model and the reasons for their choice;
- know the importance of qualities rather than looks;
- have considered how they could be a role model for others.

Resources

pictures of famous people

Activities

- Display a number of pictures of famous people around your classroom. Include a range of celebrities, sports stars and politicians, people such as Nelson Mandela, Barack Obama, Katie Price, Britney Spears, David Beckham etc.

- Read out the following statements and ask the children to choose a picture to stand by:

  I admire this person's skill.
  I admire this person's looks.
  I admire this person's humour.
  I admire this person's qualities.
  I'm impressed by what this person has achieved.
  This person is the one I most admire.

- Class discussion about the exercise:

  What did they notice?
  Were there any people that nobody stood by?
  Was there anybody who was particularly popular?

- Write the words 'role model' on the board. Ask the class to share what this means to them.

- Put the children into pairs. Ask them to discuss the people who are role models to them and why. Encourage them to think about family members, friends, relatives, teachers, celebrities etc.

- Tell the class that you will be asking for feedback about the qualities their role models show and allow them time to highlight which characteristics are important for them.

- Each pair feeds back information about their personal role models. Create a list of the qualities and characteristics on the board. As a whole class, discuss which qualities were the most important.

- Children could write a short piece about their role model explaining why this person is so important to them.

Extension activities

- Ask the pupils if they think they could be a role model for other people and who those people might be. Elicit: siblings, other relatives, peers, younger children etc.

- Children work in groups to share what qualities they think are important to be a good influence on others.

- Individuals then circle one quality they already have and one they would like to have.

- Feed back to the class.

Key Stage 2

Theme 4

Influences

Lesson 6: Fashion

Does it matter what clothes humans wear?

Intended learning outcomes

Pupils:

- have considered their own opinions about fashion;
- understand the pressure that children are under to buy particular clothing;
- have worked together in a group to design a poster encouraging children not to be influenced by designer wear.

Resources

two pictures of trainers – designer and non-designer
art materials for posters

Activities

- Play a game of Pictionary with the children using clothing and fashion vocabulary.
- Tell the class that they will be thinking about clothes and fashion in the lesson. Put 'Agree' and 'Disagree' signs at opposite ends of the classroom and explain to the children that they will hear a statement and they will need to stand on the line at the appropriate point, depending on whether they agree or disagree with the statement.

    Read out the following statements:

    I think wearing fashionable clothes is important.
    I like to wear the same as my friends.
    I always want to buy designer clothes.
    Sometimes I have been unkind to someone because of what they are wearing.
    I don't care about clothes or fashion.

- Show the class two pairs of trainers: one is designer and the other isn't. Ask the class to think about the difference between the two pairs, share ideas as a class, then ask the following questions:

  Do they think the trainers will cost the same?

  Why might someone buy one pair rather than the other?

  Generate a class discussion about why children may feel pressure to buy the more expensive pair of trainers. Include issues such as peer pressure, advertising, marketing etc.

- Class work in pairs or small groups to design a poster campaign showing children that it doesn't matter what you wear.

- Display/use for school assembly.

Influences

Lesson 7: Circle time session:
social networking

Are social networking sites the best way to stay in contact with friends?

Intended learning outcomes

Pupils can:

- listen to each other;
- contribute to a group discussion;
- take turns and co-operate with each other;
- understand the positive and negative aspects of social networking.

Resources

none needed

Activities

- This is a circle time activity. Refer to page 21 for a reminder of how to run these sessions effectively.

- *Rules for circle time:*

    Listen to each other
    Respect each other
    You may pass if you wish.

- *Name game:* Children take it in turns to say their name accompanied by a facial expression that everyone else copies.

- *Silent statements:* Read out the following statements. If the child agrees with the statement they stand up and change places with somebody else:

    I use social networking sites.
    I have a personal profile.
    I go on to the social network site every day.
    This is a good way to keep in touch with my friends.
    I sometimes worry about how my profile looks.
    People send some funny jokes and pictures.
    I saw something unkind about someone on a social network site.
    A profile gives a true picture of how someone really is.
    I sometimes say things that I wouldn't say face-to-face.
    I've seen things on the computer that were meant for older people.

- *Partner work:* In pairs, find two things that are good about social networking and two that are not so good. Feed back to the circle.

- *Open discussion:* Discuss the benefits and drawbacks of social networking that were brought up during partner work. Encourage an open class discussion in the circle by using the following prompts:

    How long do you spend on social network sites?

    Is it just for keeping in contact with current friends or do you use it to make new ones?

    Do you think the way people present themselves on social network sites is how they really are?

    Why might anybody try to be different on a social network site?

    Are the pictures or images presented on a profile important?

- *Sentence completion:* Children complete the following sentence:

    'Social network sites are . . .'.

- *Game:* Chinese Whispers – Somebody thinks of a sentence to whisper to the next person in the circle. This is passed around quickly until it comes back to the start. The final child reveals the sentence they have heard.

- *Ending:* Pass the smile.

Key Stage 2

Theme 4

Influences

Lesson 8: Toys and games

Do toys and games have an effect on young humans?

Intended learning outcomes

Pupils:

- understand that toys are sometimes gender-stereotyped and this can have an influence on the expectations of boys and girls;

- have considered the impact of computer games and how they present males and females;

- have discussed the influence of computer games, the importance of age ratings and considered the impact they may have on children.

Resources

Barbie or Bratz doll, GI Joe or Action Man
toy catalogues
scissors
glue
paper

Activities

- Show the class the boy and the girl doll. Ask the girls in the class to think of as many words as they can to describe the girl doll and the boys to do the same with the boy doll.

- Divide the board in half – girls on one side and boys on the other. Run the activity as a game so that the children take it in turns to call out adjectives for each side. Build up a list of describing words for each toy.

- Ask the children to notice the sorts of words used to describe the way the dolls look. Ask them if they think that the proportions of the dolls reflect real life. Tell them that if Barbie was a real person she would be 7 feet tall!

- Ask the children how many of them have or have had one of these dolls. What is positive about them as a toy for young children? What might be negative? Encourage the children to think about the image that these dolls project and raise their awareness of the influence they might have on children when they are so young.

- Put the children into small groups and give each group a toy catalogue, glue, scissors and three pieces of A4 paper. Ask the group to label each sheet: Boy toys, Girl toys, Toys for boys and girls. The children find toys that they think are for each gender, or both, and create a collage on each piece of paper.

- Ask the children to think about the following questions in their groups:

    Which toys are the most creative?
    Which toys are about making yourself look nice?
    Which are the most active/physical?
    Which encourage speech?
    Which are about looking after something or someone?

- Feed back and discuss as a whole class. Generate a class discussion about whether toys have an influence on young children and if that could have an impact as you get older.

- Ask the children to think about the toys they play with now. Generate a list on the board and discuss.

- Find out from the class how much time they spend playing computer games and use a voting system to discover the three most popular games for boys and girls in your class.

- In small groups, ask the children to think about what the differences are between the games that the boys like and those preferred by the girls.

- Feed back from the groups and extend the discussion by considering how females and males are portrayed in the games they play. How do the characters look, and does this reflect real life? Can the children think of reasons why there are age limits on the computer games, and is this a good thing?

Extension activity

- Ask the class to talk to older members of their families about the toys they played with when they were children.

Influences

Do you think that the stories young people hear have an impact on them?

Lesson 9: Fairy tales

Intended learning outcomes

Pupils:

- understand the way fairy stories link physical appearance to character;

- have considered how fairy stories might influence younger children;

- have created an alternative story to tell to younger children that does not link attractiveness to positive qualities.

Resources

big paper
pens and pencils
selection of fairy stories (optional)
Roald Dahl's poem – 'Little Red Riding Hood and the Wolf' (optional)

Activities

- Tell the children that they are going to think about the story of *Cinderella*. Elicit what they can remember and encourage them to tell the story around the class.

- The children work in pairs. They are given a large piece of paper which is divided in two. On one half they write the word 'Cinderella' and on the other they write 'The Ugly Sisters'. The pairs think of as many adjectives as they can to describe each of the characters.

- The children circle three from each and feed back on to the board. Ask the question: What do you notice about the way these characters look and how does that link with their qualities and personality?

- Encourage a class discussion about the link made in this story between being attractive and being a good person. Ask the children whether this reflects real life and what impact these stories could have on little children. Help them to consider what messages this story sends to children.

- The children work together to write an alternative *Cinderella* that doesn't link attractiveness with being a good person.

Extension activities

- Ask the class to think of as many fairy tales as possible. Create a list on the board.

- Put the class into groups and give each one a different story. Ask them to find the 'goodies' and the 'baddies'.

- Feed back onto the board. Think about the following questions:

  How often is the good character attractive?
  How often is the bad character unattractive?
  How often does the unattractive character live happily ever after?
  Why do many fairy stories present a similar message?

- In groups, the children create alternative stories to tell to younger children in the school (reading Roahl Dahl's story poem of 'Little Red Riding Hood and the Wolf' may help the children with ideas).

8

Transition: growing up and moving on

These lessons are aimed at children aged approximately 11, many of whom will be preparing to transfer to secondary school. Ideally, the children would have studied the other body image themes earlier in Key Stage 2. However, these lessons can also stand alone and can be taught without referring to past work.

During this theme, children are encouraged to look back over their primary school career and reflect on all the changes that have taken place both physically and emotionally. They have the opportunity to recognise and celebrate their achievements, focus on their positive physical attributes, explore their own personal journey and highlight their hopes for the future. The aim is for the children to feel positive about themselves as individuals. The lessons help them to recognise and focus on their own qualities and strengths so that they can be confident to present themselves at their new school.

For those children moving schools, there is recognition that children may be worried about the move, and some of these lessons offer the opportunity for them to share their concerns and offer support for each other.

Aims of the transition lessons

- Celebrate individuals' achievements.

- Recognise the physical changes that have taken place throughout primary school and highlight the positive aspects of those changes.

- Raise awareness of body language and how to connect positively with others.

- Consider the meaning of individuality and how important it is to be true to your identity.

- Explore concerns about moving school and develop strategies to cope with the change.

Key Stage 2

Transition: growing up and moving on

Lesson links to ECM outcomes and SEAL themes

Lessons	Every Child Matters	SEAL
1. Lifeline	Enjoying and achieving Achieving economic wellbeing	Going for goals Changes Good to be me Relationships
2. How I've changed	Being healthy	Relationships Good to be me Going for goals
3. My achievements	Enjoying and achieving Being healthy Making a positive contribution	Going for goals Good to be me
4. Worries	Being healthy Staying safe	Changes Getting on and falling out Saying no to bullies Relationships New beginnings

Lessons	Every Child Matters	SEAL
5. Going to secondary school	Being healthy Staying safe Making a positive contribution	Changes Relationships New beginnings
6. Agony aunts	Being healthy Staying safe	Changes Relationships New beginnings
7. Making new friends	Being healthy Staying safe Making a positive contribution	Relationships Getting on and falling out
8. Body image game	Being healthy Staying safe Making a positive contribution Enjoying and achieving	Good to be me Getting on and falling out Changes Relationships Going for goals

Transition: growing up and moving on

Lesson 1: Life line

Intended learning outcomes

Pupils:

■ can imagine a positive future for themselves;

■ know that their actions can have consequences for their future;

■ understand that their school life is only a short part of their whole life.

Resources

big paper
pens

Activities

■ Draw a line across the board and mark it in increments of 5.

0___5___10___15___20_____85 ___90...

■ Tell the children that this is a life line and that it is dotted at the end because they may well live to over 100.

■ Ask the children to tell you how old they were when they started nursery and primary school – also ask them to tell you when they will start and leave secondary school and mark all these ages on the life line.

■ Ask the class what they notice when they look at the line. Highlight the short amount of time that the children have at school in comparison with the rest of their lives.

■ Circle an age in the future such as 30 and ask the class to talk in pairs about what they would like their lives to be like at that time. Encourage them to consider the following questions:

What job would you like to have?
Where would you like to live?
Will you be married?
Will you have children?
What car will you drive?
What sort of holidays will you go on?
What other interests or hobbies will you have?

■ Feed back and share some ideas as a class.

- Give each child a piece of paper to make their own personal life line. They can put on any important events in their lives that have already happened as well as fill in their 'ideal future'. Some of the children may want to present this to the class.

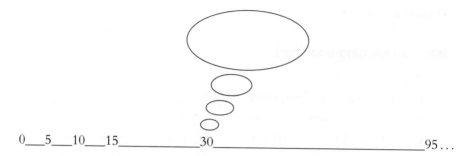

0___5___10___15_____30_____95 . . .

- Ask the children to think about what steps they will need to take, particularly at secondary school, for them to achieve their 'ideal future'.

Transition: growing up and moving on

Lesson 2: How I've changed

Intended learning outcomes

Pupils:

- understand how they have changed over time;
- have talked positively about themselves;
- have recognised and focused on their positive physical attributes.

Resources

photographs of the teacher as a baby, a young child and a teenager
photographs of the children when they were babies, in reception class and midway
through their time at primary school
paper
pens

Activities

- Show the children photographs of yourself at different stages in your life. Share what you can remember and highlight the changes that you can see in each photograph.
- Put the class into pairs and ask the children to look at the photographs of themselves as babies, in reception and at different stages in their school life. Tell them to notice all the things that are still the same about their physical appearance and those that have changed.
- Feed back some of the changes they have noticed and create a list on the board.
- Look again at the photograph of yourself and tell the class one of the changes about yourself that you are most happy about. Ask them to share with their partner a change they feel positive about. The children can decide if they want to feed back this information.
- Ask the children to make a timeline showing the photographs of themselves at different stages in their lives. Tell them to imagine the changes that will happen for them in secondary school. Encourage a class discussion about the sort of changes that will happen in their new school, eliciting physical changes as well as emotional developments.
- The children imagine how they might look in the future and draw a picture of themselves at 16 to add to their timeline.
- Ask the children to present their timeline to a partner highlighting one positive element of their appearance at each stage on the line.

Extension activities

- If your class has done the self-portraits in Key Stage 1 and 2, this will be an opportunity to look back at those pictures. The children could create self-portraits for themselves at this stage and an imagined one for the future.

- Help the class to consider all the physical differences and what has stayed the same. In pairs, encourage them to focus on each others' pictures and compliment their positive attributes.

- All of the paintings could be put into a book showing how they have changed and grown.

Transition: growing up and moving on

Lesson 3: Circle time session:
  my achievements

Intended learning outcomes

Pupils can:

■ listen to each other;

■ contribute to a group discussion;

■ take turns and co-operate with each other;

■ celebrate their achievements and those of others.

Resources

paper
pens
sheets of newspaper

Activities

■ This is a circle time activity. Refer to page 21 for a reminder of how to run these sessions effectively.

■ *Rules for circle time:*

  Listen to each other
  Respect each other
  You may pass if you wish.

■ *Name game:* Children introduce themselves and say one thing they have done that has made them feel happy. The next person does the same and then repeats what the previous person said. As it goes around the circle it becomes more difficult to remember all the things that have been said.

■ *Cross the circle:* Read out the following statements. If the child agrees with the statement, they stand up and change places with somebody else:

  I have received a swimming badge.
  I have had a certificate for work.
  I have had a sticker on my work.
  I have been in a school play.
  I have acted in a school assembly.
  I have read out my work to others.
  I have organised a game in the playground.
  I have been a good friend.

I have had a job in class.

I have been on a school trip.

I have enjoyed being at primary school.

- *Partner work:* In pairs, children discuss their achievements in primary school and what they are most proud of. Feed back to the group, either individually or for their partner.

- *Open discussion:* As a group, the class discuss all the key achievements that have been discussed. They are encouraged to think about what they hope to achieve when they move on to their next school and their hopes for the future.

- *Sentence completion:* Children take it in turns to complete the following sentence:

  'When I'm in secondary school I hope to . . .'.

- *Game:* Place some large sheets of newspaper on the floor. Tell the group that these sheets are islands surrounded by the sea. The children move around within the circle, 'swimming' in the sea. Then, when someone shouts 'Shark!', they must jump onto the newspaper. Allow the children a few goes before taking away some of the newspaper sheets. You might rip some newspaper in half to make the task more difficult. The idea is for the group to help each other stay out of the sea.

- *Ending:* Pass the smile.

Extension activity

- In pairs, the children make each other a certificate for their proudest achievement. These can then be presented in a class ceremony.

Key Stage 2

Transition: growing up and moving on

Lesson 4: Worries

Intended learning outcomes

Pupils:

- can recognise their feelings;
- know that they have changed physically and emotionally;
- understand that they already have the skills to overcome some of their worries;
- are aware that past events can be used to help them learn strategies for the present and the future.

Resources

pens
paper
envelopes

Activities

- Ask the class if they can remember their first day at school. In pairs, the children share their personal memories, then feed back to the whole group. Encourage a class discussion about how we remember important events vividly. You may want to share your own memories about your own first day at school.
- Tell the children that you want them to think back to that first day and remember what they were excited about and all the worries they had when they were starting primary school. Create two lists on the board.
- Remind the children that now they have been in school for six or seven years, they have not only physically changed but have also developed and matured emotionally. Tell the class that you want them to imagine that they could meet their younger self. Choose one of the worries and elicit from the class what they might say to that little reception child just starting on their primary school journey. What advice might they give them?
- Put the class in pairs. Ask each pair to choose three of the worries and share what they would now say to their younger selves.
- Share some ideas as a class.
- The children write a letter to themselves as reception children, giving advice and highlighting all the aspects of school they have to look forward to.
- The letters can be read out in assembly or to a younger class. They may be displayed or taken home as a keepsake.

- Ask the children to look back at the list of worries and notice any that are the same now they are going to secondary school.
- Use the letters to highlight the skills the children already have in dealing with worries that might arise from going to secondary school.
- Create a 'worry box' in the classroom. The children can put any of their own particular worries into the box and these can be dealt with at another time, either privately or anonymously as a class.

Key Stage 2

Transition: growing up and moving on

Lesson 5: Circle time session:
           going to secondary school

Intended learning outcomes

Pupils:

- can listen to each other;
- can contribute to a group discussion;
- can take turns and co-operate with each other;
- have shared their feelings about secondary school.

Resources

talking object
music

Activities

- This is a circle time activity. Refer to page 21 for a reminder of how to run these sessions effectively.

- *Rules for circle time:*

     Listen to each other
     Respect each other
     You may pass if you wish.

- *Name game:* Each child takes it in turns to tell a memory from their primary school education. They can use a talking object and pass it to another pupil asking, 'What do you remember?'

- *Cross the circle:* Read out the following statements. If the child agrees with the statement they stand up and change places with somebody else:

     I'm really looking forward to going to secondary school.
     I will miss primary school.
     I'm ready to leave primary school.
     I'm worried about fitting in.
     I think I might have to change when I'm at secondary school.
     I'm excited about making new friends.
     I'm a bit scared that I won't make friends.
     I'm worried that I won't be popular.
     I'm looking forward to all the new lessons.
     I'm worried about homework.

- *Partner work:* In pairs, discuss one thing they are looking forward to about going to secondary school and one thing they are worried about. Feed back to the circle.

- *Open discussion:* Lead a discussion with the group using the following prompts:

  What will be the same in secondary school?
  What will be different?
  What skills have you learnt in primary school that you can use to help you?
  What can you do to support each other when you go to secondary school?

- *Sentence completion:* Children take it in turns to complete the following sentence:

  'In secondary school I will...'.

- *Game:* One child chooses someone across the circle and says, 'I want [name] to copy me.' Then they do an action such as hopping, clapping in a rhythm, making a funny face etc. The partner copies. That child then chooses another child across the circle to do the same. The game continues until everyone has had a go.

- *Ending:* Pass the smile.

Transition: growing up and moving on

Lesson 6: Agony aunts

Intended learning outcomes

Pupils:

- can work co-operatively in a group;
- have considered a variety of worries;
- have shared ideas to offer advice and support;
- understand the importance of being true to themselves.

Resources

paper
pens

Activities

- Tell the class they are going to read a letter from a child who is going to secondary school. It is a girl who is worried about something and needs advice.
- Read out the following letter to the children:

  Dear Agony Aunt,

  I need help. Next year I'm starting secondary school and my friend has told me that in Year 7 you are expected to go out with someone. I don't want to have a boyfriend but feel like everyone will think I'm really young if I don't. What should I do?

  Yours truly,
  A. Pupil

- Ask the children to think about what advice they would give to the girl. Discuss as a class and create a reply on the board that suggests that she doesn't need to worry. Lots of children don't have boyfriends or girlfriends, and if someone asks, it is fine to say no. Encourage a discussion about peer pressure and the kind of rumours that make people worried about going to another school.
- Put the class into small groups and give each one a 'worry' to create into a letter for an agony aunt, e.g. I'm too small, I'm shy, I won't fit in, I have a disability, I hate my freckles and am afraid people will laugh. (You may choose to use some worries based on the fears children have put into the worry box.)

- When the letters have been written, they can be moved around the groups so that every group receives a different worry to consider. The children who receive the letter discuss what advice they would give, and bullet point ideas.

- Each group presents their problem and the advice they have given back to the class. Engage the children in a class discussion with each letter so that they are supported to think about encouraging the letter writer to be true to themselves.

- The children then write the answer to the letter.

- Ask the children to review all the important advice that they gave and create a list on the board of key things to remember at secondary school e.g. be true to your self, don't do things to impress others, talk to a friend, tell a teacher, etc.

- The children choose one of the pieces of advice that they think will be helpful to them and write it on a piece of card to be laminated like a ruler.

Extension activity

- Invite a trusted older child into the class to talk about their first experience of secondary school and to answer questions.

Transition: growing up and moving on

Lesson 7: Circle time session:
making new friends

Intended learning outcomes

Pupils:

- can listen to each other;
- can contribute to a group discussion;
- can take turns and co-operate with each other;
- have shared their feelings about friendship;
- understand strategies to make new friends.

Resources

talking object

Activities

- This is a circle time activity. Refer to page 21 for a reminder of how to run these sessions effectively.
- *Rules for circle time:*

    Listen to each other
    Respect each other
    You may pass if you wish

- *Name game:* The children take it in turns and greet the person next to them: 'Hello, [name] how are you?' The other child responds and then repeats the greeting to the next person until it has gone around the circle.
- *Cross the circle:* Read out the following statements. If the child agrees with the statement they stand up and change places with somebody else:

    I have a best friend.
    I have lots of friends.
    I sometimes like being on my own.
    I'm good at making new friends.
    I feel a bit nervous about meeting new people.
    My friends have to like the same things as me.
    I wear similar clothes to my friends.
    I have friends that are boys and girls.
    A genuine friend doesn't expect me to change.
    I'm looking forward to making new friends at secondary school.

- *Partner work:* In pairs, children discuss what a true friend is. Ask them to think about the qualities of their friends they value the most. Feed back to the group.

- *Open discussion:* As a group, the class discuss how to make a new friend. Encourage the children to think about how they might first approach another child, think about the power of body language and allow them to practise very closed and negative body language compared with open, positive body language.

  The group share ideas about what they would do and what they would say.

  Create a list of 'openers' to use when you want to connect with another child e.g. Have you done your homework? Did you watch [programme] last night? What lesson have we got next?

- *Sentence completion:* Children take it in turns to complete the following sentence:

  'A good friend is someone who...'.

- *Game:* Tell the group they will be telling a story about friendship. Start the story with the sentence, 'Once upon a time there were two friends...'. Throw the talking object across the circle to another person. They have to continue the story by adding a sentence. They then throw the object to someone else. The story ends when everyone has had a turn.

- *Ending:* Pass the smile.

Transition: moving on and changing

Lesson 8: The body image game, 'Happy to be us!'

Intended learning outcomes

Pupils:

- can take turns and express their opinions;
- celebrate their qualities and achievements;
- can identify strategies to resist body image pressures;
- feel positive about their physical appearance.

Resources

copy of the 'Happy to be us!' game
sad face cards
dice
counters

Activities

- Photocopy the 'Happy to be us!' game.
- Photocopy the sad face cards, cut up, and create a set for each game.
- You may wish to laminate the cards and the game.
- The game is designed to be played by groups of 4–6 children.
- The groups will need a dice and counters to play the game.
- Tell the children that they take it in turns to roll the dice and move their counters around the board, following the instructions when they land on each square. Remind them how important it is to respect each other's contributions.
- You may wish to discuss the game and review their learning when they have finished playing.

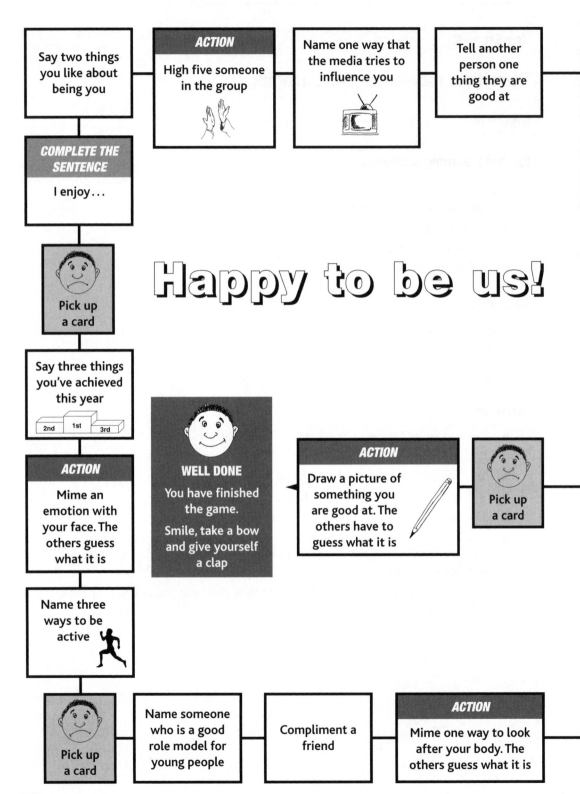

Say two things you like about being you

ACTION
High five someone in the group

Name one way that the media tries to influence you

Tell another person one thing they are good at

COMPLETE THE SENTENCE
I enjoy...

Pick up a card

Happy to be us!

Say three things you've achieved this year

2nd | 1st | 3rd

ACTION
Mime an emotion with your face. The others guess what it is

WELL DONE
You have finished the game.
Smile, take a bow and give yourself a clap

ACTION
Draw a picture of something you are good at. The others have to guess what it is

Pick up a card

Name three ways to be active

Pick up a card

Name someone who is a good role model for young people

Compliment a friend

ACTION
Mime one way to look after your body. The others guess what it is

The body image game...

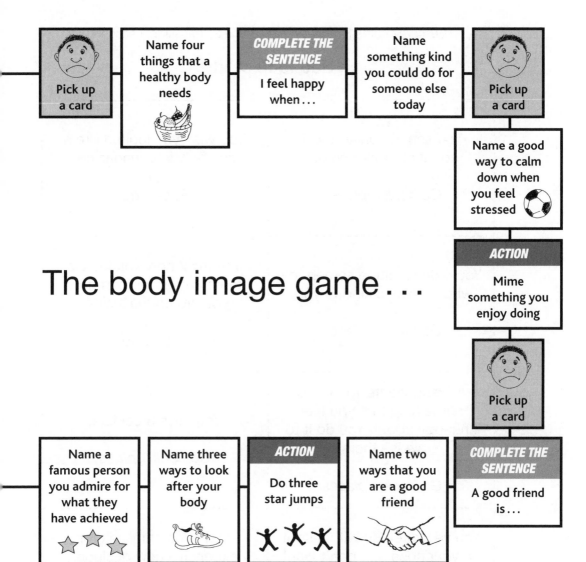

Pick up a card

Name four things that a healthy body needs

COMPLETE THE SENTENCE
I feel happy when...

Name something kind you could do for someone else today

Pick up a card

Name a good way to calm down when you feel stressed

ACTION
Mime something you enjoy doing

Pick up a card

Name a famous person you admire for what they have achieved

Name three ways to look after your body

ACTION
Do three star jumps

Name two ways that you are a good friend

COMPLETE THE SENTENCE
A good friend is...

Tell another person what you like about the way they look

Pick up a card

Say one thing you are good at

Name three qualities you look for in a friend

START

Sad face cards

You sent an unkind text about another person.

Go back 3 places

You wish you looked like a celebrity in a magazine.

Miss a go

You didn't include somebody who is always kind to you.

Go back 2 places

You think how you look is more important than how you are on the inside.

Miss a go

A friend wants you to do something that you feel unhappy about. You do it to please them.

Go back 4 places

You miss breakfast.

Go back 1 place

You've woken up with a spot on your nose and don't want to go to school.

Go back 5 places

You constantly ask for expensive new designer clothes.

Miss a go

You played a computer game meant for much older children.

Go back 3 places

You often spend 6 hours a day looking at screens.

Miss a go

Sad face cards

You tease someone about the way they look.

Go back 4 places

You think it is more important that your shoes look good rather than that they are comfortable.

Go back 2 places

You see an advert for something and immediately want to buy it.

Miss a go

You watch a film for much older children.

Miss a go

You say something mean about someone on Facebook.

Go back 3 places

You always compare your looks to your friends'.

Miss a go

You don't eat fruit or vegetables.

Go back 3 places

Friends said unkind things about another friend and you didn't stand up for them.

Miss a go

Involving parents and carers

Setting up a school meeting for parents

Parents and carers have such a strong influence on their children's body image that it is important to involve them in this topic as early as possible. Some parents and carers may feel anxious about teachers discussing body image with their children and will need to be reassured about the types of activities that will be done in school and how they can support the work at home.

When setting up a meeting, consider the following points:

- Send out a letter early to parents (example on page 162) to inform them about the planned topic and to allow them enough time to arrange to attend the meeting.

- Offer childcare or crèche facilities so that parents can attend without their children. This will allow them to air any concerns and ask specific questions that may be difficult with other children present.

- Think about the venue for the meeting in school. Use a room that is private; a classroom, for example, rather than the school hall.

- Involve a member of senior management so that parents see that this is an initiative supported by the school as a whole.

- In this meeting it is possible that parents may be concerned that they have unwittingly added to body image pressures for their children. Reassure them that nobody gets it right all the time and keep the approach positive and non-judgemental.

- Allow time for discussion and questions. Some parents or carers may want to meet with you later in confidence to discuss any particular worries about their own child.

Running a school meeting

Introduce the topic

Explain that the children will be doing some work in school that has some explicit links to their body image. Help the parents/carers to understand the importance of focusing on body image in the curriculum at this age by using some of the research information from the theory chapters 1 to 3 of this book. The YouTube references in the Resources section are also a powerful way to remind the adults about just how much media influence their children are exposed to on a daily basis.

Beliefs and values

When discussing this work with children it will be important for parents to recognise that their own body image concerns might influence how their children feel about their own appearance. It is helpful, therefore, to start with ourselves and our own attitudes. These have a powerful effect on our children and parents need to be aware of the messages they give out.

Give the parents/carers a copy of the body image quiz to help them to reflect on their beliefs about themselves. They may wish to do this in pairs or on their own.

This is not a way to make everyone feel guilty – most of us have some issues around our body image at some points in our lives. This is just an opportunity to reflect on how much emphasis we may inadvertently be placing on physical appearance. Be clear that they will not be expected to feed back any of their answers, but be prepared to facilitate any discussion that this activity may generate.

The body image curriculum

Outline the main themes of the body image curriculum. You might use the top sheets from each theme, which give an overview of each lesson and highlight the aims of the work. Be clear with parents and carers that this work is primarily about building self-esteem, encouraging the children to value who they are as individuals and celebrating their own and others' qualities. They will think about the importance of looking after their bodies and focus on what they like about their physical appearance.

The children will be introduced to the idea of influence and helped to consider what aspects of their world might have an impact on how they see themselves. The aim is to encourage the children to be more questioning and reflective about what they see around them in the media. As the adults, we need to equip the children with the tools they need to filter and manage these images and messages.

How can parents/carers help?

Research shows us that the most influential role model in a child's life is their parent or carer and it will be important for them to work in tandem with the school in order to reinforce the positive messages being taught.

Inform them that the children will be encouraged to discuss what they have learnt with the adults at home.

Give them the Top Tips sheet with a list of 'Dos' and 'Don'ts' to help them at home.

Allow time for them to read the sheet and give them the opportunity to ask any questions.

Example letter to parents

Dear ....

This term we will be working on 'Body Image' as a topic in your child's class. The aim of the work is to further develop the children's self-esteem and focus on recognising and celebrating their qualities and characteristics.

There will be specific lessons looking at the influence of peer pressure and how the media can affect how they see themselves. We will also be encouraging the children to talk to you at home about what they are learning.

A meeting has been organised for parents to learn more about the body image curriculum and for you to have the opportunity to ask any questions about the topic.

The meeting will take place on ....
at ....

If you cannot attend the meeting but would like some further information, please don't hesitate to contact me at the school.

Best wishes,

....

Body Image Quiz

Think about the following questions and answer them as honestly as you can.

1. How often do you weigh yourself?
   a) Never
   b) Occasionally
   c) Once a week
   d) Every day

2. How often do you go on a diet?
   a) Never
   b) A couple of times a year
   c) When I feel overweight
   d) I'm always on a diet

3. How often do you exercise?
   a) Never
   b) I exercise when I'm trying to lose weight
   c) Once a week
   d) Every day

4. How different is how you look from how you would like to look?
   a) Completely different
   b) Slightly different
   c) About the same
   d) Exactly the same

5. Do you find yourself comparing your body to other people's?
   a) All the time
   b) Frequently
   c) Occasionally
   d) Never

6. Do you complain about aspects of your body?
   a) All the time
   b) Frequently
   c) Occasionally
   d) Never

7. You go out for a celebratory meal with friends and eat a big meal, including pudding. How do you feel after the meal?
   a) Very guilty – I won't be able to eat for a week now!
   b) A little bit guilty – I'll have to be careful what I eat this week
   c) OK – I can't be 'good' all the time
   d) I just enjoy the fact that I've had a great night out

8. Think of three things you love about your own body.
   a) ....
   b) ....
   c) ....
   How long did it take you to come up with the list?

Think about the answers you have given to this quiz. This may give you some idea about your own body image and the variety of feelings and attitudes that we all hold around this issue.

Top Tips for parents/carers: Your child's body image

Do...

- Accept your own body size and shape.

- Listen to your children. Focus on the feelings behind their behaviour and take their fears seriously. If they are being teased at school, contact the teacher and follow it up.

- Talk positively about your child, recognising their skills and qualities.

- Offer reassurance about how your child looks.

- Encourage your child to question and challenge society's narrow 'beauty ideal'.

- When you watch television or look at magazines with your child, question the media images they see. For example, ask 'How many people do you see who look like the models in this magazine?'

- Encourage your child to express their opinions and value their individuality.

- Be active as a family; emphasise fitness, fun and enjoyment as the motivation rather than to lose weight.

- Sit down together as a family to eat a balanced diet including fresh fruit and vegetables.

- Be aware of what your child is accessing through their computer and what they watch on television.

Don't...

- Complain about your own appearance or 'ugly/fat' body parts, or at least don't share those opinions with your child.

- Make negative comments about your child's weight or appearance.

- Make negative comments about other people's physical appearance to your child.

- Over-emphasise the importance of looks.

- Crash-diet or encourage your child to diet.

- Over-emphasise the issue of food and weight.

Body Image in the Primary School, Routledge © Nicky Hutchinson and Chris Calland 2011

Resources

Website addresses

www.empoweredparents.com (advice for parents)

www.womenshealth.gov/bodyimage/kids (advice for parents)

www.bbc.co.uk/parenting/your_kids/primary_index.shtml (advice for parents)

www.kidsandnutrition.co.uk (advice for parents, encouraging a positive body image in your child)

www.cyh.com (kids' health topics, advice for children and parents)

www.b-eat.co.uk (understanding eating disorders and the impact of poor body image). Helpline no: 0845 634 1414

www.sirc.org/publik/mirror.html ('Mirror, Mirror': a summary of research findings on body image)

www.about-face.org (outlines the negative images and messages girls and women receive through the media)

www.circle-time.co.uk (Jenny Mosley consultancies)

www.timesonline.co.uk 'Skinny Barbie blamed over eating disorders' (article about the impact of Barbie on children's body image)

www.telegraph.co.uk 'Children should be taught self-esteem in schools'

(Article highlighting the importance of explicitly teaching children how to feel good about themselves)

www.childreninthepicture.org.uk (lists picture and story books that promote the inclusion of disabled children)

http://sciencewise.anu.edu.au Primary school girls worried about body image. (A research project highlighting the issue of poor body image in primary aged children)

www.wikipedia.org (self-portraits)

YouTube references

Dove – beauty pressure (shows media images that young girls are exposed to) **Parents only**

The media's effect on body image (shows painfully thin models) **Parents only**

Dove onslaught – high-definition (shows a model being made up and the image manipulated)

Dove evolution (a model's image is manipulated)

Dove commercial – 'Through her eyes' (children photograph each other celebrating their beauty)

Dove 'True colours' (highlights how many young girls are negative about aspects of their appearance)

Body image and the media (shows a variety of images from magazines)

Michael Jackson face transformation (shows the changes made by plastic surgery)

Songs

'Beautiful' – Christina Aguilera
'Freckles' – Natasha Bedingfield
'Unwritten' – Natasha Bedingfield
'True Colours' – Cyndi Lauper
'Don't Stop Believing' – *Glee* cast
'What a Wonderful World' – Louis Armstrong
'Respect' – Aretha Franklin
'The Climb' – Miley Cyrus
'Walking on Sunshine' – Katrina and the Waves
'You've Got a Friend' – James Taylor/Carole King
'Thank You for Being a Friend' – Andrew Gold
'Lean on Me' – Bill Withers

Reading books for children

Books celebrating diversity

Why Am I Different? by Norma Simon
We're Different, We're the Same by Bobbi Kates
Whoever You Are by Mem Fox
All Kinds of People by Emma Damon
All Kinds of Feelings by Emma Brownjohn
Lucy's Family Tree by Kare Halvorsen Schreck
The Skin You Live In by Michael Tyler
Pink! by Lynne Rickards
I Like Me, I Like You by Laurence Anholt and Adriano Gon
Accept and Value Each Person by Cheri J. Meiners

Books about looking after our bodies and growing up

Oh, the Things You Can Do That Are Good for You! – All About Staying Healthy by Tish Rabe
Once There Were Giants by Martin Waddell and Penny Dale

Books to boost self-esteem

The Magic Sunglasses by Auriel Blanche
You Are Who You Are by Jo-Ann D. Lefrier
Stinky the Bulldog by Jackie Valent
The Magically Mysterious Adventures of Noelle the Bulldog by Gloria Estafan
I Love My Hair! by Natasha Tarpley
Black, White, Just Right by Marguerite W. Davol
One Clever Creature by Joseph Elliss
I'm Special, I'm Me by Ann Meek
Belinda's Bouquet by Leslea Newman
I'm Gonna Like Me: Letting off a Little Self-esteem by Jamie Lee Curtis
From the Inside Out by Linda L. Lee and Jesse W. Lee
Happy to Be Me! by Christine Adams, Robert J. Butch and R. W. Alley
Oliver Onion: The Onion who Learns to Accept and be Himself by Diane Murrell
I Am a Star! – My Building High Esteem Book by Suzanne E. Harrill
A Bad Case of Stripes by David Shannon
Sink or Swim by Valerie Coulman
Tudley Didn't Know by John Himmelman
Hip Hip Hooray for Annie McRae! by Brad Wilcox
Dog Eared by Amanda Harvey
I Am a Lovable Me – Affirmations for Children by Sharon Penchina and Dr Stuart Hoffmen (affirmations)
Just Because I Am by Lauren Murphy Payne (affirmations)
I Like Myself by Karen Beaumont (affirmations)

Books about friendship

Small Acts of Kindness by James Vollbracht
The Smartest Giant in Town by Julia Donaldson
The Snow Child by Debi Glion
Standing up to Peer Pressure: A Guide to Being True to You by Jim Auer
Chowder by Peter Brown
Tobin Learns to Make Friends by Diane Murrell
Friends Learn about Tobin by Diane Murrell
The Rainbow Fish by Marcus Pfister
You're Not My Best Friend Anymore by Charlotte Pomerantz

Bibliography

Abramovitz, B. A., Chhabra, J. and Birch, L. L. (1998) Mothers' weight loss behaviours predict ideas about dieting in their five-year-old daughter. *Journal of the American Dietetic Association*, 98(9).

Altabe, M. (1996) Ethnicity and body image: quantitative and qualitative analysis *International Journal of Eating Disorders*, 23, 153-8.

BBC News Online (2007) Eating disorder in six-year-old. 27 March.

BBC News Online (2009) Children's six-hour screen day. 19 January.

Birbeck, D. and Drummond, M. (2006) Very young children's body image: bodies and minds under construction. *International Education Journal*, 7(4), 423–34.

Bryan, J. (2003) How can we learn to love our bodies? (wwwChannel4.com/health//microsites/0-9/4health/food/abe_image.html)

Compass (2006) The commercialism of childhood. (www.compassonline.org.uk)

Croft, H. (2004) Women on the front line: altered images. *Socialist Review*. June.

Cusumano, D. and Thompson, J. (2001) Media influence and body image in 8-11-year-old boys and girls: a preliminary report on the multidimensional media influence scale. *International Journal of Eating Disorders*, 29(1), 37–44.

Daily Telegraph (2010) Facebook: millions feel 'too unattractive for social networking site'. 18 March.

Daily Mail (2010) The Suri Cruise effect: how parents spend over £700 a year to help their children in style. 24 March.

Derenne, J. and Beresin, E.V. (2006) Body image, media and eating disorders. *Academic Psychiatry*, 30, 257–61.

Elliott, V. (2010) Primark withdraws padded bikini for seven-year-old girls. *The Times*. 14 April.

Field, A., Austi, S. B., Striegel-Moore, R., Taylor, C. B., Camargo, C. A., Laird, N. and Colditz, G. (2005) Weight concerns and weight control behaviours of adolescents and their mothers. *Archives of Pediatrics and Adolescent Medicine*, 159, 1121–26.

Girlguiding UK (2009) *Self-esteem: Girls Shout Out!* Attitude survey of girls aged 7–21 across the UK. (accessed online: Girlsattitudes.girlguiding.org.uk/home.aspx)

Godson, S. (2010) I don't fancy my overweight wife. *The Times*, 2 January.

Groesz, L., Levine, M. and Murnen, S. (2002) The effect of experimental presentation of thin media images on body satisfaction: a meta-analytic review. *International Journal of Eating Disorders*, 31, 1–16.

Hardy, L. (2010) From one worried mother, a passionate call to arms... It's time to stop the fashion industry destroying girls of ten like this. *Daily Mail*, 11 February.

Haywood, S. (2009) Remember Ruby? www.outofrange.net/2009/06/26/remember-ruby

Hill, A. J., Oliver, S. and Rogers, P. J. (1992) Eating in the adult world: the rise of dieting in childhood and adolescence. *British Journal of Clinical Psychology*, 31, 95–105.

Hopkirk, E. (2010) Teenage girls would consider plastic surgery. *Evening Standard*, 19 June.

Kostanski, M. and Gullone, E. (2007) The impact of teasing on children's body image. *Journal of Child and Family Studies*, 16, 307–19.

Krahnstoever Davison, K. and Birch, L. L. (2002) Processes linking weight status and self concept among girls from ages 5–7 years. *Developmental Psychology*, 38(5), 735–48.

Leitch, L. (2010) Abs fab: how the six pack took over. *The Times*, 13 January.

Lister, S. (2010) Size zero diets could put teenage girls' health at risk. *The Times*, 6 January.

Lunde, C. (2009) What people tell you gets to you: body satisfaction and peer victimization. *University of Gothenburg, doctoral dissertation*.

Maloney, M. J., McGuire, J., Daniels, S. R. and Specker, B. (1993) Dieting behaviour and eating attitudes in children. *Journal of Child Psychology and Psychiatry*, 34, 1117–24.

Ofsted (2008) Tellus 3 survey of children and young people. The Office for Standards in Education.

Papadopoulos, L. (2010) Sexualisation of young people review. Home Office.

Pettigrew, S., Pesud, M. and Donovan, R. (2009) Children's perceived and ideal body images: social marketing implications. *International Review on Public and Nonprofit Marketing*, 7(1).

Phares, V., Steinberg, A. R. and Thompson, J. K. (2004) Gender differences in peer and parental influences: body image disturbance, self-worth and psychological functioning in preadolescent children. *Journal of Youth and Adolescence*, 33(5), 420–29.

Schur, E. A., Sanders, M. and Steiner, H. (2000) Body dissatisfaction and dieting in young children. *International Journal of Eating Disorders*, 27, 74–82.

Skemp-Arlt, K., Keely, S. R., Mikat, P. R. and Seebach, E. (2006) Body image dissatisfaction among third, fourth and fifth grade children *Californian Journal of Health Promotion*, 4(3), 58–67

Stice, E., Stewart Agrras, W. and Hammer, D. (1999) Risk factors for the emergence of childhood eating disturbances: a five year prospective study *International Journal of Eating Disorders*, 25, 375–87.

TheSite. Ethnicity and body image. (www.Thesite.org/healthandwellbeing/wellbeing/bodyimageandselfesteem/ethnicityandbodyimage)

Treasure, J. L., Wack, E. R. and Roberts, M. E. (2008) Models as a high risk group: the health implications of a size zero culture. *The British Journal of Psychiatry*, 192, 243–44.

Tremblay, L. and Lariviere, M. (2009) The influence of puberty onset, body mass index and pressure to be thin on disordered eating behaviours in children and adolescents. *Eating Behaviours*, 10, 75–83.

Truby, H. and Paxton, S. (2002) Development of the children's body image scale, *British Journal of Clinical Psychology*, 41, 185–203.